Verbal Behavior in Everyday Life

Walter Weintraub, M.D., is Professor and Director of Graduate Education in the Department of Psychiatry of the University of Maryland School of Medicine. A psychoanalyst, teacher, and clinical investigator, he is the author of the book, *Verbal Behavior* (Springer, 1981), and many articles in the areas of verbal behavior, psychotherapy, and psychiatric education. A full-time faculty member of the University of Maryland since 1957, Dr. Weintraub is a member of the American Psychoanalytic Association, the International Psychoanalytic Association, and a Fellow of the American Psychiatric Association. As a consultant to the United States government, he has developed procedures for analyzing the speech patterns of world leaders.

Verbal Behavior in Everyday Life

Walter Weintraub, M.D.

SPRINGER PUBLISHING COMPANY
New York

To the women in my life:

My mother, who first taught me to decode written messages; my wife, Monique, who created a supportive work environment; and my daughter, Michèle, whose rapid and accurate work facilitated the preparation of this book.

Copyright © 1989 by Springer Publishing Company, Inc.

Springer Publishing Company, Inc.
536 Broadway
New York, NY 10012

89 90 91 92 93 / 5 4 3 2 1

Library of Congress Cataloging-in-Publication Data

Weintraub, Walter, 1925-
    Verbal behavior in everyday life / Walter Weintraub.
        p.   cm.
    Bibliography: p.
    Includes index.
    ISBN 0-8261-5790-4
        1. Psycholinguistics. 2. Personality. 3. Personality assessment.
    4. Psycholinguistics—Case studies. 5. Personality—Case studies.
    6. Personality assessment—Case studies. 7. Presidents—United
    States—Language—Psychological aspects—Case studies.
    8. Presidents—Psychology—Case studies. I. Title.
    455.W374   1989
    153.6—dc19   88-38695
                                                               CIP

Printed in the United States of America

Contents

Preface

In 1981 I wrote *Verbal Behavior*, a summary of free-speech studies I had carried out during the previous 20 years. The book dealt primarily with the relationship between syntactic or grammatical choices and personality characteristics. I wrote the book for a readership of those interested in verbal behavior research. Much to my surprise, the book aroused a certain interest in the general public. Feature articles were written about my work in newspapers and magazines. I was approached by radio and TV talk show hosts who invited me to discuss my work before unsophisticated audiences.

I was somewhat taken aback by all this unaccustomed attention. It seemed that people were fascinated by the notion that a knowledge of word selection can help us define a speaker's character.

Verbal Behavior was primarily about large populations. But I was asked by a number of readers if my method could be applied to individuals. At about the same time, I was approached by the U.S. government and asked to develop a method that could usefully apply verbal behavior analysis to the understanding of individual world leaders.

Verbal Behavior in Everyday Life brings together some of the work I have completed during the past five years. Its focus is the individual, how we go about trying to create a personality profile from unconsciously selected grammatical structures. In order to make progress in this area, it was first necessary to solve certain technical problems, notably those having to do with attribution of speech samples and the grammatical expression of emotion.

In order for the reader to judge the usefulness of my method for the analysis of individual speakers, I have chosen as my subjects the seven post-World War II Presidents. The verbal data upon which my analyses are based are public and the behavior of my subjects is sufficiently well-known for the reader to compare my profiles with his or her own knowledge of the United State's Chief Executives.

The book contains a certain amount of preliminary discussion of issues important to all of us—deception and its detection, decision making, and the language of intimacy are a few of them. The systematic exploration of these areas will occupy me during the coming years.

Readers of _Verbal Behavior in Everyday Life_ will note that the title combines the traditions of psychoanalysis and behaviorism. This is most appropriate since my research has been concerned with the precise measurement of phenomena observed while conducting a psychoanalytic and psychotherapeutic practice. I have been working within a clinical tradition that is more than 50 years old and to which I was introduced by Dr. Jacob Finesinger, the first Chairman of Psychiatry at the University of Maryland.

With the exception of Chapter 2, which is an expansion of previously published work, all data in the book are being publicly presented for the first time. I wish to thank those readers of _Verbal Behavior_ who have been kind enough to share with me their criticisms of my work. Their comments have been an inspiration to me and have stimulated several of the studies included in this book.

Acknowledgments

In the course of the preparation of this book, many colleagues have helped with their stimulating and critical comments. I wish to single out Dr. Dave Paskewitz and Dr. Michael Plaut as especially deserving of my gratitude. These University of Maryland psychologists made valuable contributions to the analysis and interpretation of the verbal data presented in this book. Without their support, my task would have been much more difficult.

PART I
Verbal Behavior and Personality Assessment

CHAPTER 1

Introduction

Recently, one of my patients—I shall call him Alvin Shuster—told me about a frustrating experience at work. A middle-aged corporate executive, Mr. Shuster had been promoted above a number of colleagues as part of an administrative reorganization. One of his first tasks in the new position was to make sure that a demoted executive, Bernard Gordon, sought his approval for certain decisions Gordon had previously made independently. Mr. Shuster reported the following phone conversation he had had with Mr. Gordon about an hour before one of our psychotherapy sessions:

MR. SHUSTER: Hello Bernie. I understand that you have been negotiating with the Underwood people for the Davis Building. Please don't commit us to anything before clearing it with me.

MR. GORDON: Congratulations on your promotion, Al. The negotiations are proceeding smoothly. I don't think there will be any problems.

MR. SHUSTER: I'm glad to hear that. The Davis Building is an important acquisition and I want to approve the terms before the deal is consummated.

MR. GORDON: Al, I understand your position completely. Unless something unusual happens, I believe that I can keep you informed every step of the way.

MR. SHUSTER: I appreciate your attitude, Bernie. Remember, I want to sign off on the deal before it's final.

MR. GORDON: Relax, Al. I'm an extremely loyal person to work with. I'm planning to check frequently with you. I don't anticipate any problems.

3

In recounting the episode, Mr. Shuster described Mr. Gordon's tone as respectful, even deferential. He could not understand why he felt vaguely dissatisfied and tired, as if he had been in a struggle. After all, he had accomplished his goal of establishing his authority over his new subordinate with very little difficulty.

Mr. Shuster, of course, was wrong. By skillfully choosing his words, Mr. Gordon had retained his autonomy, reserving to himself the right to decide the circumstances under which he would consult his new supervisor. What is more, he spoke in such an agreeable way that Mr. Shuster surrendered his authority without being aware of what had happened. Only his fatigue was a signal that all was not right.

The grammatical structure of Mr. Gordon's remarks reveals an interesting and effective style of speaking. All his responses to Mr. Shuster's comments begin with strongly positive and disarming statements. These are followed by two *qualifiers* ("I don't think," "I believe"), a *retractor* ("unless"), and two *negatives* ("I *don't* think," "I *don't* believe").

Mr. Gordon is an example of a "yes, but" obsessional speaker. Disarming and pleasant on the surface, "yes, but" speakers are extremely stubborn and controlling in their relationships with others. They can be quickly identified by their frequent use of *negatives*, *qualifiers*, and *retractors*. The "yes, but" conversationalist is one of a variety of domineering speakers we shall meet in Chapter 5. There we shall learn how to recognize and deal with them.

This brief introduction to verbal behavior in everyday life illustrates the principal theme of this book. Patterns of speech, like all complex behaviors, reflect important personality traits. Our choices of grammatical structures are not accidental but mirror significant ways of thinking and behaving. Since conversational behavior is at least moderately stressful for most people, close attention to grammatical style can tell us a great deal about how speakers cope with interpersonal stress. A detailed grammatical analysis of a speaker's remarks may also permit us to make an educated guess about the underlying forces dictating a particular verbal style.

PLAN OF THE BOOK

Verbal Behavior in Everyday Life shares with the reader some of my investigative work since 1980. The issues dealt with are those we encounter in everyday conversations.

Chapter 1 will provide the reader with enough information about my method to enable him or her to interpret the results presented in the succeeding chapters. Those readers wishing to use my method for their own research will find a completely scored verbal transcript in the Appendix.

In Chapter 2, we shall explore the intriguing subject of spontaneity in speech. We are always impressed by the ability of a speaker to talk fluently without any apparent preparation. How is this feat accomplished? Why is it that some speakers can speak extemporaneously so much more easily than others? We shall discover the phenomenon of false or pseudospontaneity and see how important a role it plays in public life. The reader will learn how to measure true spontaneity in speech transcripts.

The subject of spontaneity in speech will lead us to such interesting subjects as the public behavior of political leaders and "realistic" dialogue in the theater. We shall try to solve the problem of how politicians manage to be fluent and polished in situations that seem to be out of their control. If the reader has ever wondered how playwrights manage to transform ordinary conversation into moving dialogue, Chapter 2 may provide some of the answer.

Chapter 3 will deal with the grammar of deception and decision. These two subjects flow naturally from our study of spontaneity. We shall discover why previous efforts to define "lying" and to detect its presence in speech have proved to be so frustrating. In our discussion of decision making, we shall learn how to identify decisive and impulsive speakers as well as "wafflers," people whose ability to decide is paralyzed in stressful situations.

The grammatical reflections of expressive speech will be the subject of Chapter 4. Why do some speakers impress us as "warm," others as "dry" and "aloof?" What grammatical choices are responsible for the dramatic effect of the histrionic speaker? Why does the speech of women often sound more immediate and compelling than that of men? What is responsible for the naïveté and freshness of children's speech?

In Chapter 5, we shall explore the special language of intimacy. Analyzing real life conversations, we shall dissect the processes of introduction, engagement, and disengagement. We shall note the ways in which our grammatical choices serve as a barometer of our rapport with others. Special attention will be given to distinguishing true intimacy from pseudointimacy or familiarity. We shall learn about the verbal reflections of a disintegrating relationship.

Studying the language of intimacy will lead naturally to a consideration of the special ways that families and groups communicate. What purposes are served by the elliptical devices and neologisms that characterize family and group languages? How does slang develop and what determines whether or not slang expressions become part of the standard language?

Certain aspects of intimate behavior involve controlling relationships. In Chapter 5, we shall look at how people use conversational techniques to control and dominate others. What role do forms of address play in domineering behavior? How do competitive speakers use turn-taking rules to control conversations? The reader will learn some strategies that are useful in combatting aggressive conversationalists.

In Chapter 6, we shall learn how to apply verbal behavior analysis to the study of personality. What methods of data gathering are to be used? How large a sample is necessary for the analysis of a single individual? Which traits should be studied in order to obtain a picture of a living, functioning human being?

Finally, in Chapters 7 through 14, we shall apply the lessons we have learned about everyday verbal behavior to the speaking styles of U. S. Presidents since World War II. Analyzing Presidential news conferences, we shall sketch personality profiles of seven U. S. Presidents. We shall examine the verbal reflections of Eisenhower's self-confidence as well as his purposeful use of befuddlement. John F. Kennedy's special relationship with the press will be explored. How was his unique charm mirrored in his grammatical choices? The broad, manipulative style of Lyndon B. Johnson will come to life in his extraordinary conversational behavior with White House reporters. The impressive organizational and pedagogical skills of Richard Nixon will emerge in our examination of his news conferences. Nixon's remarkable sensitivity to criticism and its disintegrating effects upon his Presidential performance will be noted.

Gerald Ford's brief term as modern America's only nonelected Chief Executive will afford us the opportunity of identifying verbal habits we have come to associate with tentativeness and passivity. Jimmy Carter's press conferences will highlight his ambivalent relationship with the White House press corps. Highly competitive and sensitive to criticism, Carter used his encounters with the journalists to demonstrate his intellectual superiority to them. Our final Presidential subject, Ronald Reagan, will show how a leader can establish a friendly relationship with reporters despite wide ideological differences. Reagan's successful courting of the press will be carefully analyzed. How is Reagan's undeniable charm reflected in his verbal behavior? How does he resemble and differ from the other post-World War II Presidential charmer, John F. Kennedy?

In our various Presidential analyses, we shall focus primarily upon verbal style, although use will also be made of other communication modalities when appropriate. Sufficient information about experimental procedures has been included in the text to allow the reader to share the excitement of discovery.

GRAMMAR AND PERSONALITY

How do we go about identifying grammatical structures that reflect important personality traits? In my book, *Verbal Behavior: Adaptation and Psychopathology*, I described in detail a method of associating styles of speaking with patterns of thinking and behaving. Two examples will demonstrate how my method works.

The first illustration concerns a man with problems of impulse control. He acts without considering the consequences of his behavior. As a result, he often finds himself regretting his actions and trying to undo their harmful effects. How might this impulsive trait be reflected in our subject's speech? We would expect him to blurt out ill-considered remarks and then attempt to take them back or qualify them in some way. How would this tendency be mirrored in his grammatical choices? We would anticipate that our subject would make frequent use of "adversative" expressions, such as "but," "however," and "nevertheless." A number of years ago, a colleague, Dr. H. Aronson, and I published a report showing that a group of hospitalized, impulse-ridden psychiatric patients *did* use significantly more adversative expressions than a group of normal control subjects (Weintraub & Aronson, 1964). Similar results were later obtained from a group of binge-eaters, individuals who impulsively consume large quantities of food and then try to undo the consequences of their eating in various ways (Weintraub & Aronson, 1969).

Let us take as our second example an individual with compulsive, ritualistic behavior. Such a person feels compelled to perform repetitive, apparently senseless acts, such as washing his hands over and over again or checking repeatedly to see if his door is locked before retiring for the night. If our subject attempts to resist his compulsion, he becomes extremely anxious and cannot long maintain his resolve. Since compulsive persons are "logical" to a fault, they must provide themselves and others with reasons to justify their repetitive acts. We would, therefore, expect their speech to contain numerous explanatory expressions, such as "because," "therefore," and "in order to." A study Dr. Aronson and I published confirmed this expectation. A group of compulsive psychiatric patients did, in fact, use significantly more explanatory expressions than a normal control group (Weintraub & Aronson, 1974). Similar results were found with a group of delusional patients who demonstrated a strong need to justify unconventional beliefs (Weintraub & Aronson, 1965).

While reading the two clinical examples above, the reader was, perhaps, struck by the similarity of the grammatical structures studied to defense or coping mechanisms described by psychoanalytic clinicians. Adversative expressions appear to reflect the mechanism of "undoing," explanatory expressions that of "rationalization." In fact, almost all the categories I use in my verbal analyses have been described by clinicians as reflecting important ways of dealing with psychological stress.

Collecting Verbal Data

If we wish to use verbal mannerisms as a way of determining how an individual copes with stress, it is important to gather samples of speech under moderately stressful conditions. Subjects exposed to minimal or extreme levels of stress will not provide us with the verbal data we are seeking. An example will illustrate this point. Suppose we wished to test a baseball player's ability to catch fly balls. How would we go about it? We would not hit balls beyond human reach since nobody, not even the most skillful player, could meet such a challenge. Nor would we hit balls directly to our ballplayer since almost anyone could catch them. To properly test a player's catching skills, we would hit difficult but catchable fly balls. I have found that requiring a subject to speak uninterruptedly for a period of 10 minutes on any subject he or she wishes is a difficult but manageable task for most individuals between the ages of 5 and 85. Normal as well as emotionally disturbed people can speak uninterruptedly for 10 minutes. Researchers use the term "free speech" to refer to verbal samples gathered under experimental conditions I have just described.

Development of Verbal Styles

How are differences in verbal styles acquired? The reader may be surprised to learn that we do not yet know the answer to this question. To some extent, the way in which we make our grammatical choices appears to be influenced by the verbal styles of the important people in our early environment, notably parents, siblings, and friends. But this is far from being the whole story. We know that children growing up in the same family, attending the same schools, and sharing the same groups of school and neighborhood friends can develop markedly different verbal styles. It is possible that verbal mannerisms are, in part, hereditary (Munsinger & Douglass, 1976).

Despite the many studies carried out on language development, we still do not know how children begin to speak. According to the so-called nativist theory of language acquisition, proposed by Chomsky (1964) and Lenneberg (1964), the structures and functions of the nervous system essential to the learning of language are present at birth. The opportunity for interaction with speaking individuals is the only necessary environmental contribution.

It appears likely that differences in verbal styles are evident as early as age two or three and continue, with some developmental modifications, into adulthood. I made it a practice to record verbatim samples of my children's speech from their very early years. Upon reaching adulthood, they have had no difficulty matching their grown-up ways of speaking with their childhood verbal samples. My daughter, Michele, believes her adult verbal style contains many characteristics that were already present at the age of 3.

Studies carried out on the free speech of children and adolescents indicate rapid and dramatic changes in the choice of grammatical structures associated with increasing age. The frequency of occurrence of the personal pronoun, "I," tends to vary inversely with the pronoun, "we," for example, the predominance of the one or the other depending upon the extent of group participation in the particular age group. Thus, children between the ages of five and seven, who are relatively self-preoccupied, make great use of "I" and relatively little use of "we." Pre- and early adolescents, aged 9 to 14, on the other hand, show the opposite pattern, reflecting their greater involvement in group activities (Weintraub, 1981).

The analysis of free speech samples has shown interesting differences between males and females. Female subjects make greater use of explanatory and adversative expressions as well as the pronoun, "me." In the case of explanatory expressions, the gender differences begin as early as age five (Weintraub, 1981).

TRANSFORMATIONAL GRAMMAR
AND VERBAL STYLE

Let us consider, for a moment, the question of why different people use different grammatical structures to convey the same message. "John loved Mary" and "Mary was loved by John" are two grammatically correct ways of saying the same thing. Transformational grammarians would say that they constitute different surface structures derived from a common deep structure. Every language is considered to have transformational rules that allow its speakers to say the same thing in different ways. Although, in our example, the two sentences are identical in meaning, they differ noticeably in style. When we compare the verbal styles of different individuals, we are, in a way, comparing preferences for transformational rules. Why a particular person chooses one rather than another grammatical structure is related, in my view, to personality factors. We might suppose that the sentence, "John loved Mary," may be too blunt and assertive for certain people who would prefer the more passive and softer, "Mary was loved by John." In fact, some of my previous work indicates that inactive or helpless psychiatric patients do have a preference for certain passive grammatical structures (Weintraub, 1981).

SOME PRACTICAL USES OF VERBAL
ANALYSIS

A method associating personality with verbal style has a variety of uses. In clinical work, verbal behavior analysis has obvious applications to diagnosis and to the assessment of treatment response. My method, for example, has been used to monitor the course of psychoanalytic therapy (Natale, Dahlberg, & Jaffe, 1978). As I have indicated above, developmental changes in language behavior from early childhood through old age have been traced by means of verbal analysis. A particularly interesting application of my method has been in the area of psychohistory. I have analyzed the Watergate transcripts and have sketched the personality profiles of the four principal conspirators, Richard Nixon, John Ehrlichman, H. R. Haldeman, and John Dean. All the above studies have been fully described in my book, *Verbal Behavior*.

It is in the area of psychopathology that my method has found its most important use. During the past 20 years, Dr. H. Aronson and I have published reports comparing the speech patterns of impulsive, compulsive, delusional, depressed, binge-eating, and alcoholic persons with those of normal individuals (Weintraub & Aronson, 1964, 1965, 1967, 1969, 1974; Weintraub, 1981). In all cases, we have been able to demonstrate patterns of grammatical usage that reflect the symptomatic behavior and thinking of these groups.

A METHOD OF VERBAL BEHAVIOR ANALYSIS

Thus far I have succeeded in isolating a number of verbal categories that are stable over time, are easily measured, and appear to reflect clinically significant behavior. The following is a list of the categories we shall be discussing in this book:

1. I
2. we
3. me
4. negatives
5. qualifiers
6. retractors
7. direct references
8. explainers
9. expressions of feeling
10. evaluators
11. adverbial intensifiers
12. nonpersonal references
13. creative expressions
14. rhetorical questions
15. interruptions

As I have clearly stated in *Verbal Behavior*, I claim no priority for the observation and description of the verbal mannerisms we shall be using. All have been noted and reported in anecdotal ways by clinical investigators. What my colleagues and I have attempted to do is to define the verbal reflections of psychological coping mechanisms so that naive judges can score them without extensive knowledge of lexical meaning. For readers interested in using the method for their own research, I have included a scored speech sample in the Appendix.

I. All occurrences of the pronoun, *I*, whether used alone or as part of a contraction, are counted. Very high or low scores may indicate, respectively, self-preoccupation or detachment. A moderate use of *I* probably reflects a healthy ability to commit oneself in thought and action while maintaining an adequate degree of autonomy. An infrequent use of *I* indicates an avoidance of intimacy, commitment, and candor.

We. All occurrences of this pronoun are scored, whether used alone or as part of a contraction. Unlike *I*, which almost always refers to the speaker, *we* can include both the speaker and individuals known to the speaker. Leaders sometimes use *we* in the "imperial" sense. ("We shall go to Paris to meet the French President.") In such cases, the pronoun is really being used as an *I* and should be so scored.

We can be used in impersonal ways. In such instances, the pronoun does not refer to individuals known to the speaker. ("We won World War II.") When both *we* and *nonpersonal references* scores are high, the speaker is probably using the pronoun in a detached, impersonal way; a low *nonpersonal references* score accompanied by a high *we* score indicates a more intimate use of the pronoun.

A moderate *we* score suggests a healthy capacity to recognize and to collaborate with others. When the frequency of *we* is high and that of *I* is low, avoidance of intimacy and commitment is indicated, particularly if the *nonpersonal references* score is also high. A certain ratio of *I* to *we* scores may be a useful measure of self/object differentiation.

Me. All occurrences of this pronoun are scored. *Me* appears to be the most intimate of the personal pronouns. Since it is generally used as the object of action verbs, *me*, when used frequently, may reflect passive strivings.

Negatives. All negatives, such as "not," "no," "never," and "nothing," are scored. *Negatives* may be associated with the coping mechanisms of negation and denial. A high *negatives* score may, therefore, indicate a problem in reality testing. On a more superficial level, the frequent use of *negatives* suggests a stubborn, oppositional trait.

Qualifiers. This category includes (a) expressions of uncertainty ("*I think* I'll go to the ball game today"); (b) modifiers that weaken statements without adding information ("That old house is *kind of* spooky"); and (c) phrases that contribute a sense of vagueness or looseness to a statement ("Then we enjoyed *what you might call* an evening of relaxation").

Qualifiers are almost always uttered before the complete verb is spoken. The message is, therefore, discounted before it is transmitted. When they occur frequently, *qualifiers* indicate a lack of decisiveness or an avoidance of commitment. The use of *qualifiers* has also been said to increase with anxiety (Lalljee & Cook, 1975).

A very low frequency of *qualifiers* conveys a dogmatic flavor to speech. In Chapter 2, we shall see that *qualifiers* are extremely important in measuring the degree of spontaneity in speech.

Retractors. In this category, all expressions that partially or totally retract immediately preceding statements are scored. Expressions containing such adversative conjunctions as "but," "although," "however," and "nevertheless" almost invariably cancel preceding remarks. ("John is obnoxious *but* he has contributed a lot to the organization.").

The frequent use of *retractors* suggests a difficulty in adhering to decisions already taken and imparts to a speaker's verbal style a flavor of impulsivity. Unlike qualification, which precedes and delays decision, retraction usually follows verbal action already consummated.

Although the inordinate use of *retractors* suggests a different style of behavior, moderate amounts of retraction in discourse reflects the capacity for mature reconsideration, flexibility in judgment, and openness to a broad range of possibilities. As in the case of qualification, speech without retraction has a certain barren and dogmatic flavor.

Direct References. In this category, I score all explicit references to (a) persons present and listening to the speaker's remarks ("I am happy to see you members of the press in such rare form today"); (b) the conditions under which the speaker is delivering his remarks ("Due to a previous engagement, I have only a half-hour to address you today"); (c) the physical surroundings ("It's a pleasure to meet you in such a beautiful auditorium").*

Frequent *direct references* may indicate that the speaker is having difficulty talking and wishes to divert the audience's attention from what he or she is struggling to say to the speaking situation itself. This tends to happen in impromptu speaking situations. Speakers

---

* An important rule in the scoring of this category is that consecutive *direct references* are not counted separately. If a subject, for example, discusses the tape recorder for five minutes without interruption, only one *direct reference* is counted; no more *direct references* are scored until an intervening statement is made on some subject other than the speaking situation, the audience, or the physical surroundings.

who use many *direct references* are sometimes manipulative, sometimes simply unable to understand and abide by agreed-upon speaking procedures. The latter frequently occurs in the case of small children or adults with severe psychopathology.

The complete absence of *direct references* may suggest extreme shyness, a difficulty in engaging the audience. Detached and aloof speakers frequently have low *direct references* scores.

Explainers. I score as an *explainer* any expression that (a) provides a reason or justification for an action, thought, or attitude. ("I dislike Roy *because* he is always criticizing people"); or (b) indicates a causal connection of any kind ("*Since* a large crowd is expected at the stadium, additional police will be required"). Causative conjunctions and phrases almost always are used as *explainers*, for example, "because," "as," "since," "in order to," and "therefore."

Explainers are frequently used for purposes of rationalization. Not all explaining, however, is rationalizing. I assume that excessive rationalizing tendencies may be revealed by a high frequency of occurrence of *explainers* in spontaneous speech. Speech samples that are almost devoid of *explainers*, however, may appear concrete, dogmatic, and insensitive.

Expressions of feeling. In this category, I score all expressions in which the speaker describes him or her self (either alone or as part of a group) as experiencing or having experienced some emotion. The range of scorable feelings is broad and includes the following: attraction-aversion; like-dislike; satisfaction-dissatisfaction; pleasure-displeasure; hope-despair. Other *expressions of feeling* that I count are suggestive of fear, anger, and desire. The following are scorable *expressions of feeling*: (a) "I *love* classical music"; (b) "Your birthday card *pleased me* very much"; and (c) "We *were disgusted* by his boorish behavior."

I do not score impersonal references to feelings, such as, "It was a terrifying incident." Expressions of interest, physical sensations, and conditional feelings are not scored, for example, "I would be delighted to attend if invited."

Speakers who use few *expressions of feeling* frequently convey an impression of aloofness. Those who use feeling words to an extreme may impress their listeners as insincere and histrionic. In Chapter 4, we shall learn that emotion can be expressed by a number of categories, of which *expressions of feeling* is only one.

Evaluators. All expressions of judgment in the following areas are scored: (a) goodness-badness, for example, "He's the *best* worker in the organization"; (b) usefulness-uselessness, as in, "Your idea *won't work*"; (c) right-wrong, for example, "It is *sinful* to steal"; (d) propriety-impropriety, as in, "You *should not* dress that way for a wedding"; (e) correct-incorrect, as in "You have the *right* answer"; (f) pleasant-unpleasant, for example, "It's *nice* to be on vacation in June."

Expressions of judgment in the following areas are *not* scored since they are usually conflict-free: (a) easy-difficult; (b) interesting-dull; and (c) industrious-lazy. *Evaluators* are not scored when used as quantifiers, as in "That's a *good-sized* bed."

In my experience, high scores in this category often reflect the existence of a punitive conscience. Almost all psychopathological states are characterized by a significant use of *evaluators*.

Adverbial Intensifiers. A new category, *adverbial intensifiers*, includes all expressions containing adverbs that increase the force of a statement. "I *really* like Sam" and "She is *so* beautiful" are examples of such expressions. Frequent use of *adverbial intensifiers* indicates histrionic tendencies. People who exaggerate tend to dramatize events and often see the world in black and white terms. The development and uses of this category will be examined in detail in Chapter 4.

Nonpersonal References. To score this category, divide all clauses into "personal" and "nonpersonal." A "personal" clause is one whose subject refers to a person or persons conceivably known to the speaker. Clauses having the speaker as subject are also considered to be "personal." All other clauses are scored as "nonpersonal," with the exception of those preceding indirect questions, which are not scored in either category. Anatomical parts of individuals, references to animals, the use of universal subjects, and impersonal pronouns are all scored as "nonpersonal."

The final nonpersonal references score is obtained by dividing the number of nonpersonal references by the sum of nonpersonal and personal references and multiplying the quotient by 1000.

Clinical experience suggests that an almost exclusive use of impersonal subjects in clause construction may reflect the avoidance of intimacy and responsibility. Infrequent use of nonpersonal references may indicate a certain preoccupation with oneself, one's immediate family, and associates.

The following examples illustrate the rules governing the scoring of statements in this category: (1) In the statement, "I think I'll go to the ball game", "I think" is not scored (precedes indirect quotation); "I'll go to the ball game is scored as "personal." (2) "Everybody likes ice cream" is scored as "nonpersonal." (3) "One has to drive carefully in heavy traffic" is scored as "nonpersonal."

Occasionally Used Categories

The final three categories—all introduced since the publication of *Verbal Behavior*—are used too infrequently by most speakers to permit statistical comparisons. I have found them, however, to be revealing of certain personality characteristics. Their use will be discussed from time to time in our analysis of Presidential speech patterns.

Creative Expressions. In this category, I score all expressions that include (a) any original use of language, such as neologisms or unusual combinations of adverbs and adjectives ("a fitfully red sky"); (b) original metaphors; and (c) wit. I assume—although there is no strong evidence to support my belief—that creative individuals use more of these expressions during extemporaneous speech than ordinary speakers.

Rhetorical Questions. This category includes all questions that are clearly meant to arouse and engage an audience. No answers to the questions are expected and would, indeed, be inappropriate. The use of rhetorical questions indicates an aggressive and engaging approach to an audience.

Interruptions. Referring more to conversational behavior than to verbal style, this category includes all attempts on the part of a speaker to interrupt a listener who may be asking a question or making a statement. Frequent use of this category suggests domineering behavior on the part of the speaker.

Conversion of Raw Scores to Final Scores

For nonpersonal references, we have learned how to convert raw scores to final scores on page —. For all other categories, we multiply the raw score by a corrective figure. The corrective figure is obtained by dividing 1000 by the number of words in the speech sample and rounding the result off to three places after the decimal point. In the Appendix, the complete scoring of a speech sample, including conversion from raw scores to final scores, is demonstrated.

Verbal Categories—Mean Values

The following scores reflect the performance of psychologically well-adapted adult individuals speaking extemporaneously in free speech experiments:

Category	Score
I	45–50
We	5–10
Me	2–3
Negatives	11–14
Qualifiers	9–12
Retractors	6–7
Direct References	1–2
Explainers	5–7
Expressions of Feeling	6–9
Evaluators	9–11
Adverbial Intensifiers	12–14
Nonpersonal References	400–500
Creative Expressions	1–2

We now have enough tools to begin our journey. Although our procedures are relatively simple, there are many categories and the reader will find it necessary to refer from time to time to the information given in this chapter. Let us now begin with a subject of interest to all speakers and listeners, the measurement of spontaneity in speech.

CHAPTER 2

The Grammar of Spontaneity

THE IMPORTANCE OF ESTIMATING SPONTANEITY IN SPEECH

As a psychiatrist and psychoanalyst, I have long been aware of the clinical importance of spontaneity. Psychotherapy, after all, is concerned with changing behavior and feelings, and this goal is more easily accomplished when new associations are forged between ideas and emotions. Few clinicians would contest the proposition that fresh connections are facilitated in a therapeutic environment that fosters patient spontaneity. The basic rule of free association in psychoanalytic treatment is designed, in part, to promote verbal spontaneity. Yet many patients, fearful of being overwhelmed by internal stimuli, come prepared for their therapy sessions. In extreme cases, a patient may arrive with written notes or with a list of topics to discuss. Even when there are no written notes or lists, therapists may suspect preparation if the patient's "free associations" sound too fluent, his choice of words too elegant, his logic too cogent. "Insightful" statements showing evidence of preparation may be dismissed by therapists as not genuine. Progress in therapy, as reflected in decreased patient defensiveness, is generally mirrored by a noticeable increase in verbal spontaneity.

My interest in measuring spontaneity in speech, however, was stimulated less by my work as a psychotherapist than by a project in the field of political linguistics. In today's world, governments are frequently overthrown by revolutionary leaders whose past

18

is shrouded in mystery. In order to deal with such leaders, it is important to be able to accurately assess their styles of leadership, their levels of impulsivity, their propensity for aggressive behavior, and their probable reactions to crisis situations.

In attempting to predict the future behavior of these revolutionary leaders, we must rely primarily upon recorded speeches and occasional transcribed press conferences. Psycholinguists can then attempt to develop personality profiles based on the leaders' verbal behavior.

But how can we tell whether or not a given leader actually composed the remarks attributed to him? Even if we can be sure that he uttered the words, how can we be certain that they were not written by a speechwriter and read or memorized by the leader? Clearly, a personality profile that is derived from a speechwriter's composition may not tell us much about the character traits of the leader in whom we are interested.

ATTRIBUTION OF SPEECH SAMPLES

Attribution of a sample of speech is greatly simplified if the speaker's style is already known. As Spencer and Gregory (1964) have put it, "It may be sufficient, if evidence of authorship is required, to use a computer to determine quantitatively the density in a given text of one or two specific linguistic features. . . . Or we may identify the style of a writer by referring simply to his preference for certain words or his predilection for a particular clause structure" (pp. 90–91). John F. Kennedy, for example, often used such expressions as "in my judgment," "of course," and "as you know." Preferred linguistic choices are highly characteristic and allow us quickly to solve problems of attribution. This method of attribution has been successfully used by investigators trying to determine the authorship of disputed literary works. The interested reader is referred to the fascinating research of A.Q. Morton, British classical scholar, minister, and computer expert. In his book, *Literary Detection*, Morton (1978) applies the science of stylometry to certain cases of disputed authorship with very interesting results.

But how can we solve problems of attribution if there are no previous speech samples with which to compare a speaker's remarks? It occurred to me that one possible approach would be to measure the level of spontaneity in the speaker's comments. If I could demonstrate that a sample of speech showed little evidence of preparation, I could safely attribute its composition to the speaker. Evidence of careful preparation, on the other hand, would leave open the possibility that persons other than the speaker helped author the remarks in question.

For psycholinguists interested in personality evaluation, estimating spontaneity in speech is important for another reason. Public speakers know that unprepared remarks are delivered under conditions of greater stress than prepared comments. The psychiatric interview is designed, in part, to assess a patient's ability to cope with stress by including questions for which the respondent could not have possibly prepared. When attempting to analyze personality from spoken remarks, I prefer the give and take of an unrehearsed news conference to the careful delivery of a polished speech. Psychological conflicts and important character traits are more easily revealed in human interactions that the speaker cannot easily control.

The Problem of Attribution in Psychobiography

In my book, *Verbal Behavior*, I attempted to show the usefulness of verbal behavior analysis for psychobiographical research. By applying my method to the Watergate transcripts, I was able to sketch personality profiles of the four principal participants, Richard Nixon, H.R. Haldeman, John Ehrlichman, and John Dean. These profiles defined a number of personality traits observed in the subjects' public behavior (Weintraub, 1981).

Because of the unique circumstances surrounding the recording and transcription of the Watergate conversations, we can be reasonably sure of the identity of the speakers and of the spontaneity of their remarks. Psychobiographers are rarely so fortunate. They must frequently contend with problems of attribution. Did a certain historical figure really compose the statements attributed to him or were they spoken or written by somebody else? A technique that would allow us to gauge the spontaneity of transcribed speeches and written documents, such as letters and diaries, would be of great use to biographers and historians.

INDICATORS OF SPONTANEITY

Before discussing previous attempts to measure spontaneity in speech, let us be sure that we know exactly what we mean by "spontaneity." In this chapter, I shall use the expression "level of spontaneity" to refer only to the amount of preparation that has preceded a speaker's remarks. An almost complete absence of spontaneity will be assumed to exist when a speaker reads a written statement. I say "almost complete absence" because the speaker may misread the statement and reveal something of himself in so doing. Next comes the recitation of memorized material. Here, forgetting is possible and the need to improvise may arise. A much greater degree of spontaneity is found when a speaker discusses a subject he or she has thought about but has not committed to memory. Such a performance is called "extemporaneous." "Impromptu" remarks constitute the highest degree of spontaneity. Here, the speaker comments about a subject or subjects to which he or she has not given systematic thought.

Once I had decided to study the problem of spontaneity in speech, I searched the literature to see what other investigators had discovered. I found that certain researchers studying the nonverbal aspects of speech had concluded that spontaneity is associated with the position and length of pauses in the speaker's clauses. According to these investigators, when a pause occurs within rather than at the end of a clause, it probably indicates that the speaker is having difficulty retrieving words and phrases from his long-term memory store (Mercer, 1976). Such pauses are far more likely to occur in the speech samples of unprepared speakers and may, therefore, be associated with spontaneity.

To measure the lengths of pauses in samples of speech, researchers must have access to electronically recorded reproductions of the speakers' remarks. Psychobiographers and historians usually must work with transcribed written materials. They therefore require verbal measures of spontaneity. I was surprised to learn that there have been no systematic attempts to study the verbal reflections of spontaneity in speech.

AN ACCIDENTAL DISCOVERY LEADS
TO AN HYPOTHESIS

A possible way of measuring spontaneity in speech occurred to me as a result of an experiment I had conducted many years ago. In order to compare the grammatical structure of spoken and written language, I had asked 14 medical student volunteers to provide 10-minute samples of extemporaneous monologues and five pages of free writing. In both the written and spoken parts of the experiment, the students were instructed to communicate on any topic or topics they wished. When the protocols were scored and analyzed for the verbal categories described in Chapter 1, I found only one significant difference between the written and spoken samples. The students used more qualifying phrases, such as "I think," "sort of," and "probably" when speaking. In interpreting the results of this speaking versus writing experiment, I concluded that the volunteers were under less pressure to communicate continuously when writing than when speaking. Although a research technician was present during both parts of the experiment, the students apparently found it easier to stop writing while collecting their thoughts than to pause during their monologues. Using qualifying phrases permitted them to avoid silence while retrieving words from their long-term memory storage.

I was quite excited by the idea that I had, perhaps, discovered a verbal marker for spontaneity in speech. My next step was to look carefully at the speech samples of the approximately 300 subjects, both normal and emotionally disturbed, that I had collected over the previous 20 years. Examining those transcripts having few or no qualifying phrases, I ascertained that most of them had been recorded by volunteers who, when asked to speak extemporaneously for 10 minutes, recited memorized material. One subject, an instructor in the U.S. Army, repeated an obviously memorized speech on the topic of military government.

Before describing an experiment designed to test the hypothesis that qualifying phrases constitute a marker for spontaneity in speech, I want to review with the reader the category, *Qualifiers*. In Chapter 1, I noted that this category includes expressions of uncertainty and vagueness as well as words and phrases that weaken a speaker's statements without adding information. *Qualifiers* almost always appear before the verb has been spoken. When used frequently, *qualifiers* make the speaker appear tentative and unsure of him or herself. Although experimental subjects differ among themselves in the extent to which they use qualifying phrases, I had found the category to be of little use in distinguishing groups of emotionally disturbed individuals from each other or from normal volunteers. I retained the category in my verbal system because I was confident that it measures a fundamental way of thinking and behaving. It appeared that my faith in the category's usefulness was finally to be rewarded.

EXPERIMENT I: TESTING THE HYPOTHESIS THAT QUALIFYING PHRASES REFLECT SPONTANEITY IN SPEECH

Ten freshman medical students, five men and five women, who were participants in a special psychiatry program, were asked to respond for one minute to each of 10 questions. Five of the questions were given to the students 30 minutes before the recording session. The subjects were told to prepare answers to these questions although no written notes were allowed in the studio. The other five questions were answered in an impromptu fashion, without previous knowledge of the subject matter. The experiment was designed to compare extemporaneous with impromptu speech. The hypothesis to be tested was that impromptu speech, the more spontaneous of the two, would contain significantly more qualifying phrases.

The research technician asking the questions was seated behind a one-way mirror and was not visible to the student volunteers. The questions were all of a manifestly neutral nature, such as, "What is your favorite activity?," "What are your favorite foods?," "What is your neighborhood like?" and so on. The students were not informed about the purposes of the study. The order of presentation of the questions was controlled so that half of the students began the recording session with a "prepared" question and half with an "unprepared" question. Questions that were "prepared" for half the volunteers were "unprepared" for the other half. All the students were asked the same 10 questions.

Ten 1-minute samples were collected from each of the 10 students. The samples were transcribed and scored for each of the following 10 verbal categories: *negatives; qualifiers; retractors;* the pronouns *I, we,* and *me; nonpersonal references; expressions of feeling; explainers;* and *evaluators.*

The results clearly supported the hypothesis. Only one category, *qualifiers,* distinguished "prepared" from "unprepared" responses. All 10 subjects used more *qualifiers* during their unplanned responses. No other category came close to distinguishing extemporaneous from impromptu answers. There were no significant sex differences in any of the categories (Weintraub & Plaut, 1985).

The results of the student experiment clearly indicated that qualifying phrases may be a verbal marker for spontaneity in speech, at least when used to distinguish extemporaneous from impromptu remarks. The next step was to see if this finding could be usefully applied to historical or psychobiographical material. I decided to see if different levels of spontaneity in the communications of U.S. Presidents could be distinguished by the frequency of occurrence of qualifying phrases.

EXPERIMENT II: LEVELS OF SPONTANEITY IN PRESIDENTIAL MESSAGES

Each year the United States Government Printing Office publishes a volume called *Public Papers of the Presidents of the United States.* Cumulatively, these books contain in verbatim form the public remarks of all U.S. Presidents since World War II and provide students of verbal behavior with Presidential communications of different degrees of preparation. Of the various Presidential messages, answers to reporters' questions during news conferences are among the most spontaneous. Opening remarks preceding the question and answer periods generally involve more preparation than answers to questions. Formal speeches, such as inaugural addresses and special messages to Congress, are the most carefully prepared Presidential communications.

If the frequency of occurrence of qualifying phrases is a measure of spontaneity in speech, this fact should be reflected in the different forms of Presidential messages. To test this hypothesis, I collected samples of three forms of oral communication from the seven post-World War II Presidents, beginning with Dwight D. Eisenhower and ending with Ronald Reagan. The three kinds of messages included: (1) answers to reporters' questions during Presidential news conferences held in the first year of office; (2) opening remarks preceding the question and answer periods during Presidential news conferences held in the first year of office; and (3) the first term inaugural address for each of the seven Presidents. In the case of Lyndon B. Johnson, the first address before a joint session of Congress was used since no formal inaugural address accompanied the swearing-in ceremonies in 1963.

After computing the number of *qualifiers* per 1000 words, I made a statistical comparison of the three kinds of Presidential messages. The results showed that there were significant differences in the hypothesized direction (Weintraub & Plaut, 1985).

WHY WE USE QUALIFYING PHRASES

Let us see what sense we can make of the results of the two experiments I have just described. In the student experiment, the volunteers were asked to answer each of 10 questions with a 1-minute answer. We can suppose that the student subjects, wishing to comply with the spirit as well as the letter of the experimental instructions, were under considerable pressure not to use silence to cope with the stress of the procedure. When asked questions for which they had not prepared answers, the volunteers used qualifying phrases to fill time while searching their memories for suitable words with which to convey their ideas. We have reason to believe that speakers try to preserve the unity of their clauses even when speaking spontaneously. We have already noted that qualifying phrases tend to occur at or near the beginning of clauses. This probably means that the speaker has not been able to think ahead sufficiently to produce fluent speech without the help of *qualifiers*. His speech production system is working at the limit of its capacity.

Factors Limiting Speech Production

But what limits the capacity of the speech production system? It is certainly not the neuromuscular constraints upon articulation. We rarely speak at our maximum possible speed, even less so when talking spontaneously. (Children under the age of seven *do* speak more slowly than older children and adults (Weintraub, 1981). This may be due to neuromuscular immaturity.) When speaking extemporaneously or in an impromptu fashion, we are more likely to be limited by either a lack of ideas or by a difficulty in putting thoughts into appropriate language. The frequency of qualifying phrases can be seen as a gauge of the difficulty in retrieving memories from long-term storage and in encoding them into acceptable language. In both the student experiment and the study of Presidential messages, the frequency of occurrence of *qualifiers* decreased as the amount of preparation increased.

It is likely that the use of qualifying phrases reflects more than just the lack of familiarity with the material being discussed. Even when time of preparation and familiarity with the material have been controlled for, individuals still differ significantly among themselves in the degree to which they use qualifying phrases (Weintraub &

Aronson, 1962). We must take into account a person's *natural felicity for speaking* (Horowitz & Newman, 1964). For reasons we do not yet understand, some people seem to be quicker than others in retrieving and encoding ideas from long-term memory storage.

In order to account for this difference in retrieval and encoding speed, certain researchers have proposed the interesting idea that a speaker has at his or her disposal two kinds of long-term vocabulary stores. One, the larger of the two, consists of systematically stored words and is termed a *lexicon*. Retrieval of words from the *lexicon* requires a certain amount of "searching time." In addition to the *lexicon*, there is a smaller *topicon*, which is an idiosyncratic "desk top" long-term store of potentially useful and more readily available material—ready-made phrases—essential for fluent speech. According to this model, the need to pause within clauses or to use qualifying phrases arises when one's topicon is exhausted and the need to search the lexicon arises. A fluent speaker is one with a large *topicon* (Mercer, 1976). As we shall see later on, when we discuss pseudospontaneity in political discourse, what appears to be a natural felicity for fluent speaking is often contrived, a result of careful planning.

Since both pauses and qualifying phrases seem to serve similar purposes, is it possible that different individuals have a predilection for one or the other of these speech habits? Do speakers who pause within clauses more use fewer qualifying phrases? No well-designed experiment has been carried out comparing the use of *qualifiers* with the number and lengths of pauses within clauses. A number of years ago, I was able to demonstrate that there is no relationship between the use of qualifying phrases and pauses of more than five seconds in the transcripts of extemporaneous speakers (Weintraub & Aronson, 1962). These results, however, may not be applicable to shorter pauses, which probably serve other purposes (Siegman, 1978). If a negative relationship between qualifying phrases and brief pauses within clauses were shown to exist, we might speculate that individuals who pause rather than qualify have a greater tolerance for silence when conversing with others.

OTHER USES OF QUALIFYING PHRASES

It is likely that qualifying phrases reflect more than the process of retrieval and encoding ideas from long-term memory storage. The impression that extensive qualification leaves on the listener is one of hesitation and tentativeness. It is quite possible that the frequent use of *qualifiers* indicates indecisiveness as a personality trait of the speaker.

The speaker's level of anxiety should also be taken into account when interpreting the meaning of qualification. Although experimental support is lacking, I think it likely that people who are stressed by public speaking use more qualifying phrases than those who are comfortable addressing others. When sufficiently intense, anxiety can affect any cognitive function, including the retrieval and encoding of memories from long-term storage.

Emotions other than anxiety may affect the use of qualifying phrases. Strong feelings, such as anger and enthusiasm, tend to reduce the conflictual quality of speech. Much of verbal ambivalence, which reflects the consideration of two sides of a question, is created by the use of *qualifiers* and *retractors* ("I *think* you are correct *but* there is something to be said for your opponent's point of view"). When under the influence of strong positive or negative emotion, speakers tend to see the world in all-or-nothing, black and white terms and use few *qualifiers* and *retractors*. Several years ago, I was able to demonstrate an inverse relationship between extreme anger and the use of *qualifiers* and *retractors* (Weintraub, 1981). A study of the characters of James Joyce's *Ulysses* showed that strong erotic feelings tended to reduce the frequency of occurrence of *qualifiers* and *retractors* (Steinberg, 1973).

QUALIFYING PHRASES IN MESSAGES OF DIFFERENT DEGREES OF SPONTANEITY

The results of the student experiment indicate that impromptu speech contains more qualifying phrases than extemporaneous speech. Our study of the three forms of Presidential communication shows an inverse relationship between preparation and *qualifiers*. Table 2.1 presents the average use of qualifying phrases by speakers and writers in all the forms of verbal expression I have studied. The reader will note the impressive decrease in the use of *qualifiers* as we go from lesser to greater degrees of preparation.

Assessing spontaneity in speech and writing is important in a variety of everyday situations. In the rest of this chapter, we shall consider the role of spontaneity in theatrical expression and political discourse. But first let us look at the use of *qualifiers* in normal individuals of different ages.

TABLE 2.1 Number of Qualifiers per 1000 Words for Verbal Samples of Decreasing Spontaneity

Unprepared answers to questions (student experiment)	20.7
Presidential news conferences (answers to questions)	11.5
Free speech[a]	10.6
Prepared answers to questions (student experiment)	9.7
Free writing[b]	8.1
Presidental news conferences—opening remarks	4.9
Presidential speeches	0.9

[a] Subjects asked to speak for 10 minutes on any topic or topics they choose.
[b] Subjects asked to write five pages on any topic or topics they choose.

AGE AND FLUENCY

Up to this point, we have discussed spontaneity in the speech of normal adults. But what about children and the elderly? Do the verbal reflections of spontaneity in *their* speech differ from those of young adults? Do the immature or deteriorating functions of retrieval and encoding associated respectively with childhood and old age lead to different expressions of spontaneity?

When children between the ages of five and seven are asked to talk on any topic or topics they wish for a period of 10 minutes, they speak significantly fewer words than adults and older children (Weintraub, 1981). Their silences are often prolonged and they sometimes resort to the recitation of memorized material. When they do speak in a genuine extemporaneous manner, young children use qualifying phrases. They speak much more slowly than older subjects, a phenomenon that is probably due to the incomplete development of the cognitive processes of retrieval, encoding, and articulation.

We hear a lot about children's "spontaneity," but what is really meant by that expression? I believe that we are referring less to children's grammatical choices than to the unpredictable quality of their verbal and nonverbal behavior. Small children do not obey adult rules of conversation. Compared to most adults and older children, they don't sit or stand still when speaking, may not stick to the subject being discussed, don't always follow turn-taking rules, may use certain words in idiosyncratic ways, and often ask socially inappropriate questions. The conversation of small children is strongly influenced by immediate needs and desires. It is not until they have reached the age of 9 or 10 that most children's conversational behavior begins to resemble that of adults.

What about our senior citizens? It is generally assumed by researchers that memory suffers after the age of 65. One possible way that elderly speakers have of compensating for this loss of memory is to "buy time" by using qualifying phrases and pauses. Speech samples I have collected from volunteers over the age of 65 suggest that they do not, in fact, use significantly more pauses and *qualifiers* than younger subjects. They seem to cope with age-related loss of memory by resorting to the repetition of familiar material, a practice that does not strain the speech production system beyond its capacity. When asked to speak uninterruptedly for 10 minutes, elderly subjects tend to choose autobiographical themes that are replete with familiar anecdotes. They maintain the same degree of verbal fluency as younger speakers do by avoiding unfamiliar topics (Weintraub, 1981).

Is there any evidence that children and elderly individuals use *different* qualifying phrases than do adults between the ages of 18 and 45? No. Although children do have a somewhat different lexicon than adults, they use the same small group of qualifying phrases.

SPONTANEITY IN THE THEATER

Tomorrow and tomorrow and tomorrow
Creeps in this petty pace from day to day,
To the last syllable of recorded time;
And all our yesterdays have lighted fools
the way to dusty death. Out, out brief
candle! Life's but a walking shadow; a
poor player that struts and frets his hour
upon the stage, and then is heard no more;
it is a tale told by an idiot, full of
sound and fury, signifying nothing.

The reader will recall that Macbeth's famous soliloquy in Act V, Scene V of Shakespeare's *Macbeth* is delivered immediately after he learns about the death of his wife (Black, 1937). Profoundly philosophical, the soliloquy contains no qualifying phrases. It is delivered as a polished statement, not as a real-life verbal response to a tragic event. In Shakespeare's most famous play, *Hamlet*, the hero is portrayed as paralyzed with indecision. Yet he uses only one qualifying phrase in his famous "To be or not to be" soliloquy, one of literature's most celebrated statements of ambivalence. These two examples are quite typical of Shakespeare's monologues. I sampled a number of Shakespeare's famous soliloquies and found an average of two qualifying phrases per 1000 words, about 20 percent of what one would expect in truly spontaneous monologues.

It is true that Shakespeare was writing in a different era and the great poet was describing the reactions of heroic, larger-than-life individuals to momentous events. Their monologues should not be judged by ordinary standards. What about the dialogue of more recent playwrights, particularly those celebrated for the realism of their work? I chose eight twentieth-century U.S. playwrights and analyzed the first 1000 words of dialogue from among their most famous plays with the results shown in Table 2.2 below:

TABLE 2.2

Author	Play	Qualifiers
Edward Albee (1962)	*Who's Afraid of Virginia Woolf?*	2
Maxwell Anderson (1935)	*Winterset*	2
Lillian Hellman (1939)	*The Little Foxes*	7
Arthur Miller (1949)	*Death of a Salesman*	2
Eugene O'Neill (1956)	*Long Day's Journey into Night*	2
Thornton Wilder (1938)	*Our Town*	4
Tennessee Williams (1945)	*The Glass Menagerie*	3
Herman Wouk (1954)	*The Caine Mutiny*	4

Although not a carefully controlled study, my survey of representative U.S. plays suggests that the sampled playwrights used fewer qualifying phrases in their dialogues than would be expected in real life conversations. The spontaneous Watergate conversations, for example, average about 10 *qualifiers* per 1000 words.

Because he has been acclaimed for the realism of his dialogue, Ernest Hemingway seemed to be a good novelist to investigate. I analyzed the first 1000 words of his post-World War I classic, *The Sun Also Rises* (1926). They contain only three qualifying phrases.

The astute reader may complain that the first 1000 words of a literary work's dialogue may not be representative of the speech habits of a play's or novel's characters. To deal, in part, with this anticipated objection, I analyzed the entire dialogue of Eugene O'Neill's autobiographical play, *Long Day's Journey into Night*. The number of qualifying phrases per 1000 words for each of the four leading characters are as follows:

Tyrone	1.8
Mary	2.0
Edmund	1.6
Jamie	4.5

Once again we note that O'Neill's use of qualifying phrases is far less than what one would expect in real-life conversations. It is unlikely, I believe, that literary artists known for the realism of their fictional conversations cannot create dialogue that accurately reflects real-life conversations. No matter how realistic he or she may wish to be, every author must maintain a certain dramatic pace or lose the attention of the audience or readership. A play or novel that contained as many as 10 *qualifiers* per 1000 words of dialogue would be experienced as tedious by the theater-going or reading public. As Spencer and Gregory (1964) have noted, "Characters in plays and novels never talk quite like people do in life" (p. 88). The genius of the "realistic" novelist or playwright is that he or she can create the illusion of real-life conversations without reproducing the mumbling and stumbling that constitute the dialogues of most living individuals.

PSEUDOSPONTANEITY IN POLITICAL DISCOURSE

In the spring of 1958, France was going through its worst political crisis since World War II. Frustrated by the inability of a succession of parliamentary governments to maintain control of Algeria, French overseas military leaders were in revolt against the central government in Paris. Rumors of an invasion of the capital by rebellious paratroopers spread throughout Paris. It soon became clear that only one French citizen could heal the nation's political wounds and unite his country behind one foreign policy. Cries were heard for the return to power of World War II hero, General Charles DeGaulle. Living in self-imposed political isolation in his hometown of Colomby-les-deux-Eglises, DeGaulle indicated a willingness to assume power on the condition that he could rewrite France's constitution to allow for a presidential rather than a parliamentary system of government. The General called a press conference for May 18th during which he explained his views to the French nation.

DeGaulle's news conference is surely one of the most remarkable of its kind ever held. Speaking without notes, he briefly and cogently outlined his views of France's problems and his prescription for their resolution (DeGaulle, 1958). One of modern France's greatest writers, DeGaulle sprinkled his opening remarks with memorable expressions. He spoke of his past actions constituting a "moral capital" upon which France could draw in its moment of crisis. Referring to his withdrawal from active political life, DeGaulle grandly described himself as "a man who belongs to nobody and (therefore) belongs to everybody" (p. 12).

But it was the question and answer period that provided the news conference's real drama. Asked to comment upon the situation in Algeria, DeGaulle replied, "That [overseas French] population has seen that the present system established in Paris cannot solve its problems. More than that, it has recently seen that system turn toward (good) offices from abroad. . . . It sees in Paris crisis succeed to crisis, powerlessness powerlessness, the same representatives of the same parties mixing indefinitely in the same ministerial posts without anything clear, precise and effective ever coming out of it. . . . And then the [French] Algerians cry, 'Long live DeGaulle,' as Frenchmen do instinctively when they are in the depths of anguish or on the heights of hope" (p. 12).

Questioned about "the procedure" of his possible return to power, he answered, "I reply that if DeGaulle should find himself delegated with exceptional powers for an exceptional task at an exceptional time, that could not obviously be done according to the usual procedure. . . . It would be necessary to adopt a procedure that would also be exceptional. . . . When events speak loudly and there is agreement on substance, procedures can have considerable flexibility" (p. 12).

The final question dealt with fears that DeGaulle might "attack public liberties" were he to assume power. Looking contemptuously at the reporter who posed the question, the General asked rhetorically, "Have I ever done so? On the contrary, I restored them when they had disappeared. Is it credible that at the age of 67 I am going to begin a career as a dictator?" (————).

Even after translation, the student of verbal behavior is impressed by the power of DeGaulle's rhetoric, the elegance of his style, and his complete command of the interview situation. A careful perusal of his remarks during the question and answer period reveals no verbal evidence of qualification. In a moment of crisis,

DeGaulle showed himself to be fearless, decisive, and ready to lead France into an era of peace and stability.

As we shall see later in Chapter 7, no U.S. President since World War II has been able to conduct himself with comparable sureness and authority during news conferences. Did Charles De-Gaulle possess a unique command of language that enabled him to retrieve and encode spontaneous answers to reporters' questions with uncommon fluency and refinement? No. His performance was the result of very careful preparation. Journalists were required to submit their questions well in advance of the news conference and the General memorized the answers to those questions he chose to answer. DeGaulle also rehearsed the accompanying gestures to achieve the desired rhetorical effects. The result was first-rate polit-ical theater rather than spontaneous discourse.

Theodore Roosevelt as Political Actor

One of the United States's most charismatic Presidents, Theodore Roosevelt well understood the importance of pseudospontaneity in arousing and manipulating an audience. In his autobiography, *A Child of the Century* (1954), journalist Ben Hecht described Roosevelt's technique in great and loving detail.

The day Roosevelt and his Bull Moose supporters bolted the Re-publican Party at the Chicago Convention in 1912 the colorful leader was revealed at his best. Roosevelt's delegates left the Coli-seum, where the Republican Nominating Convention was being held, and gathered at Orchestra Hall, two miles away. They sat there for two hours listening to speeches and waiting for their hero to arrive. Hecht was present in Roosevelt's hotel suite where Teddy was "tossing whiskey after whiskey down his gullet" while pretend-ing to write a speech. He smiled at the reporters, "drew pictures of comic elephants on the note paper, opened a second bottle of whiskey and wrote nothing" (p. 171). After having his fill of whiskey, much to the consternation of his political advisors, Roosevelt left the hotel, entered Orchestra Hall, and walked down the center aisle. "The knowledge that Teddy had not only arrived but *was in their midst* smote the assemblage all of a sudden, as if a firecracker had exploded under all their seats" (pp. 172–173).

Roosevelt's supporters, three thousand strong, leaped to their feet and gave out a roar that lasted for seven minutes.

> I saw him stand, his empty note pages in hand, grinning at the dervishes in
> front of him. . . . Teddy raised his hand for silence. I was for an instant

horrified. . . . No hero ever checks an ovation. It is only the near-heroes who are afraid the ovation will not last long enough who raise a pusillanimous hand for silence.

But I had misjudged our Teddy. He would as soon have thought of stopping the roars of love as of shooting down his grandmother. Our hero had raised his hand—but not for silence. He had raised it to throw the empty sheets of note paper in the air, to show his disciples that so overcome was he by their adoration that he was not going to speak to them from any notes. He was going to speak—when they allowed him—from a grateful and overflowing heart.

The scraps of empty note paper, tossed violently into the air, fluttered down around his head and as they fell the roar deepened, took on new and wilder instrumentation. And another three minutes of bedlam bulged the walls.

LEADERSHIP AND SPONTANEITY

It is obvious why a leader, anxious to convey an impression of strength and decisiveness, would want to purge his speech of qualification. To do so, however, requires preparation. Many public speakers, including great orators like Winston Churchill and Franklin D. Roosevelt, were able to inspire millions of listeners by reading their speeches on the radio. Television allows public speakers to *appear* to talk spontaneously through the use of teleprompters or cue cards.

The reader can convince him or herself of the lack of genuine spontaneity in political discourse by following any electoral campaign from beginning to end. At the start, as issues are being raised and defined, the candidates hesitate, punctuate their statements with numerous qualifiers, and make costly mistakes. In the course of the campaign, as the same issues are debated over and over again, the candidates develop categorical positions, find the "right words" with which to express their opinions, and begin to use the same phrases again and again in their speeches. As election day nears, the candidates are usually able to offer smooth, fluent responses, free of hesitation and qualification, to most questions raised by reporters and audiences.

DOES SPONTANEOUS VERBAL
FLUENCY EXIST?

At this point, the reader may be wondering whether there is such a thing as true verbal fluency. Are the witty and urbane conversationalists we see on television and listen to on the radio speaking spontaneously or have they simply mastered the art of fooling an audience into believing that they are? My observations have lead me to conclude that while several sentences of spontaneous and fluent ad-libbing are possible, lengthy impromptu remarks free of qualification and hesitation are extremely rare. In the more than 20 years I have been studying speech habits, I have listened very carefully to hundreds of speakers. They have included experimental subjects with no training or experience in public speaking as well as some of the most articulate speakers in the world. None could calmly discuss questions for which they had not prepared without hesitation or qualification. The reader is invited to judge for herself by comparing a lecturer's verbal behavior while delivering a speech with his responses to questions from the audience following the talk. If the answers to the questions appear to be smooth and articulate, try asking an "off the wall" question for which the lecturer could not have possibly prepared. Evidence of hesitation and qualification will appear almost immediately. The same is apparently true for witty conversationalists. While brief, creative, and spontaneous rejoinders are possible, extended humorous remarks can be assumed to be, to some degree, prepared.

SUMMARY

We have now reached the end of our chapter on spontaneity in speech. What began as an attempt to estimate the degree of preparation in a speaker's remarks has taken us far afield. We have become acquainted with other uses of a previously neglected category, *qualifiers*. We have studied its significance in political discourse and in the theater. In the next chapter, we shall consider two important areas of everyday verbal behavior that are to some extent related to the use of qualifying phrases—deception and decision making.

CHAPTER 3

Deception and Decision Making

VERBAL BEHAVIOR AND DECEPTION

Few aspects of human behavior have aroused more public interest than lying. Uniquely human, its manifestations and motivations have been explored by writers for centuries. As old as lying have been the attempts of listeners and observers to devise methods of detecting deception. Despite the interest of government and industry in lie detection, reliable techniques of uncovering falsehood continue to elude our grasp. The complexity of the task of lie detection begins to become apparent when we attempt to define "lying."

Searching for a Definition of "Lying"

If we define "lying" as knowingly telling a falsehood, we immediately run into difficulties. How do we deal, for example, with a metaphor like "It's raining cats and dogs," an exaggeration like "You look 20 years younger tonight," or a sarcastic comment like "Thanks a lot for losing my book!"? Even if we exclude these examples, since most people understand that they are not to be taken literally, obstacles remain. There is the vexing problem of "truth in the real world" versus truth in the world of fantasy.

If asked, "Who was the first wife of David Copperfield?", readers of Charles Dickens would promptly reply, "Dora." But David Copperfield and Dora never existed. They are fictional characters, figments of Dickens' imagination. Yet stating that Dora was David Copperfield's first wife would be universally regarded as a truthful remark. So the world of the writer must, like metaphor, hyperbole, and sarcasm, be exempted from the customary definitions of "lying" (Dolezel, 1980).

This act of deference to the literary artist does not end our task of defining "lying." There is still the problem of *personal truth* in the real world. Everyone has a private way of perceiving the world that is different from that of all other individuals. Investigators have demonstrated again and again that five persons viewing the same incident will report five different versions of what happened. These versions, let me assure the reader, will differ not only in inconsequential details but in matters of substance. Sports fans, for example, frequently observe umpires and referees disagree among themselves when calling a ball "fair" or "foul." Even television replays of disputed calls have not entirely solved this problem since the replays themselves are viewed differently by different observers.

The phenomenon of two or more observers interpreting an event differently is not due entirely to the imperfection of our sense organs. It appears that we have been prepared to observe and remember in a certain way by temperament and previous experience. Two children growing up in the same family may describe early childhood events in radically different ways. What was a kind, loving mother to one may have been a cold, manipulative woman to the other. Each sibling may be passionately convinced of the reality of his or her portrait of mother. Each can corroborate his or her impressions with "evidence." Neither sibling can be said to be lying. We shall have more to say about *personal truth* when we discuss the detection of lying.

Even if we limit our discussion of lying to situations where the facts are not in dispute, we are not out of the woods. It seems that most people do not regard the simple telling of an untruth as lying. A falsehood told out of ignorance is not, in the opinion of the majority, a lie (Coleman & Kay, 1981). It must be uttered with the intention to deceive. Nor is telling an obviously ill patient that he is looking well considered "lying" by most people since the listener knows the truth and realizes that an act of kindness is intended.

At this point we are close to the dictionary definition of "lying." It is the deliberate telling of an untruth for the purpose of deception. And yet even this definition will not satisfy everyone. Questionnaires designed to identify the most commonly accepted definition of lying have elicited data suggesting that many respondents require that a liar benefit in some way from a falsehood. Even a purposeful deceptive remark may not be considered "lying" if it is uttered for the purpose of helping or protecting another individual (Coleman & Kay, 1981).

It would be gratifying if we could be done with the task of defining "lying" and get on with the problem of detection. There are still, however, some complications to unravel.

Lying by Telling the Truth. It appears that under certain circumstances we can lie without telling a falsehood. How is this possible? Consider the following example. Henry wants to buy a surprise birthday gift for his wife, Carol. He puts on his coat and walks to the door. "Where are you going?" asks Carol. "I have to go to the drug store to get some shaving cream," answers Henry. He does, indeed, go to the drug store for shaving cream but also passes by the florist to arrange to have a bouquet sent to Carol. No falsehood has been told. Henry has deceived Carol by withholding information. Did he tell a lie? Many would say, "Yes." Some would reply that Henry's behavior, although intended to deceive, should not be called "lying" because it had no harmful or serious consequences.

There are, of course, many examples of "lying by telling the truth." Consider the following: Employee Smith's secretary asks for a day off. Not wanting to take responsibility for her action but unwilling to arouse her displeasure, Smith replies, "Make sure that your work is completed." Thinking she has her supervisor's permission, the secretary finishes her work and takes a day off. Smith's boss learns of the secretary's absence and demands an explanation. Smith truthfully denies that he gave his secretary permission to take the day off. He has, however, deceived both his boss and his secretary.

The Silent Liar. We all know it is possible to lie without saying anything, as in the following example: Professor Jones tells a small group of students an unflattering anecdote about Professor Brown. Student Green repeats the remark to Professor Brown, who writes to Professor Jones, demanding an apology. Professor Jones confronts the student group and asks, "Who told Professor Brown what I said about him the other day?" Silence greets his question. Student Green says nothing. Professor Jones continues, "I suppose the person is not in the room." Student Green has lied without saying a word.

Our Final Definition of "Lying"

Listed in the order of importance are the following ingredients of "lying:" (1) The purposeful telling of a statement that the speaker believes to be false. (2) The falsehood is told with the intention to deceive. (3) The statement *is* actually false. Some would add a fourth element, that (4) the false statement should have "nontrivial" consequences. Those concerned with the consequences of lying would not consider "fishing stories" and similar exaggerations to be lies, since the consequences *are* trivial (Coleman & Kay, 1981).

THE PROBLEM OF LIE DETECTION

The detection of lying by verbal or nonverbal analysis has proved to be an extremely complicated task. Why? Let us consider the most systematic attempt to detect deception, the so-called lie detector. This is a machine that records certain physiological reactions of a subject whose truthfulness is being evaluated.

The use of the polygraph in lie detection is based on the assumption that the deceiver will experience increased anxiety at the moment of deception. The increased anxiety will supposedly manifest itself in one or more changes in the internal state of the body, which will be reflected in the polygraph's readings (Hocking & Leathers, 1980).

But why should a liar experience increased anxiety at the moment of deception? There are several possible reasons. The subject may be in conflict over deceiving the listener, may feel guilty about having participated in the events being asked about. Another possible reason is the fear of the consequences of being detected. It is likely that a liar who has committed illegal acts for a "higher purpose," such as the welfare of his or her country, will not experience acute anxiety at the moment of deception. Such a person may pass a lie detector test with flying colors!

People whose "personal truth" is in conflict with observable facts are a special problem for the science of lie detection. According to Jeremy Campbell (1982),

> Studies of witnesses describing what they think they remember about an accident suggest that the brain can construct the event under the influence of the questions it is being asked. . . . People tend to interpret new information in the context of their previous knowledge. . . . We reconstruct information when retrieving it from memory. . . . The past is unconsciously adjusted to suit what the rememberer knows and expects in the present. (p. 226)

Campbell believes that unconscious reconstruction of memory may enable someone to make untrue replies to questions and still pass a lie detector test.

Another psychological phenomenon may complicate lie detection. It appears likely that "an untruth told repetitively over a period of time may become increasingly believable and acceptable as fact to both the person who tells it and the person who is told" (Ford, King, & Hollender, 1988). At least three women have succeeded in convincing part of the public—and, perhaps, themselves!—that they are Anastasia, daughter of Czar Nicholas II of Russia. Two of these women, and probably all three, are liars. Yet all seem convincing and might very well pass a lie detector test. They might not experience the autonomic arousal responsible for detection.

How Innocent Subjects May Fail a Lie Detector Test

Certain individuals who are not liars may become sensitized to various topics. Let me give an example. In the practice of psychotherapy, I sometimes encounter patients who are pathologically jealous or who have spouses suffering from this condition. Unjustified accusations may be made about alleged misbehavior, often with great anger and hostility. The unjustly accused mate will begin by denying the accusations and will try to reason with the pathologically jealous spouse. If the accusations continue, as they usually do, the beleaguered spouse may gradually begin to alter his or her behavior in order to "prove" that he or she is not guilty of the allegations. A married man I once treated in psychotherapy actually trained himself to look straight ahead when strolling with his wife in order to avoid her jealous outbursts. (She would angrily accuse him of looking at other women.) It is quite possible, I believe, that this patient might have failed a lie detector test had he been asked about the behavior to which his wife's outbursts had sensitized him, even though he was completely innocent of her accusations.

Studying Deception in the Laboratory

Attempts to discover the verbal and nonverbal reflections of deception in the laboratory have generally proved to be disappointing. There are several reasons for this. First of all, most experimenters tell their subjects to knowingly lie about a particular matter. The volunteer thus has permission to practice deception, a state of affairs that does not usually exist in real-life. Once authority to deceive has been given, the physiological responses that produce the effects we are trying to measure are less likely to occur.

Another problem in deception experiments is the absence of serious consequences associated with discovery. We have already noted that fear of the consequences of lying may be necessary to produce the acute anxiety so important in lie detection. Volunteers in a laboratory experiment have enough trust in the investigator to realize that participation is safe no matter how intimidating the instructions may be. If the subjects did not have this trust, they would not volunteer in the first place.

Despite some methodological shortcomings, there have been some interesting attempts to design deception experiments that *do* build consequences into the procedure and apparently succeed in generating sufficient anxiety to influence language choices. Dulaney, for example, found that liars use fewer words, fewer different words, and fewer past tense words when compared to subjects who are not lying. Male volunteers supposedly use a greater number of sentences in the indicative mood and fewer subjunctives when lying (Dulaney, 1982).

The Grammar of Spontaneous Lying. Spontaneous deception occurs when the deceiver is caught in a compromising situation and has to improvise to get out of it. According to Paul Ekman (1985), liars caught in the act betray themselves in two ways. They may "leak" the truth with subtle changes of voice, body movements, and choice of words, or they may give "deception" clues that suggest lying without revealing the truth.

Ekman offers a number of telltale signs of lying that appear to reflect arousal of the autonomic nervous system. The reader will recall that this is the same physiological mechanism responsible for changes measured by the lie-detecting polygraph. Ekman believes, for example, that dilated pupils, rapid breathing, a heaving chest, sweating, and frequent swallowing are reliable signs of lying. He also lists a number of voice changes that seem to reflect the impact of arousal on delicate laryngeal mechanisms. Among them are higher voice pitch, faster speaking rhythm, speech errors, and pauses. Other speech characteristics associated by Ekman with lying include slips of the tongue; tirades; and indirect, evasive speech. He provides his readers with a long list of nonverbal, gestural clues to deception that are not a major concern of students of verbal behavior.

It is important to note that much of what Ekman has observed and described applies only to people who have not had time to prepare their lies. They have been caught in embarrassing situations and are trying to talk their way out of their difficulties by improvising deceptive stories. With the possible exception of denial of wrong-doing, there does not seem to be any particular pattern of verbal behavior associated with spontaneous lying.

Denying Wrongdoing. Lying in order to deny wrongdoing is one of the commonest forms of deception and appears to have recognizable grammatical characteristics, such as the frequent use of *negatives, adverbial intensifiers,* and *personal pronouns.* The following example, taken from Dwight D. Eisenhower's September 30, 1953 news conference, well illustrates the grammar associated with denial of wrongdoing. Martin P. Durkin had just resigned as Secretary of Labor and had accused the President of double-crossing him on a promise to amend the Taft-Hartley Labor Law, a charge that apparently had some basis in fact (Ambrose, 1984). The following exchange took place between Associated Press correspondent Marvin L. Arrowsmith and President Eisenhower:

> *Mr. Arrowsmith:* I do not know whether your earlier remark on the labor situation applies to this or not, but I have been requested to ask you. As you know, former Secretary of Labor Durkin said that you broke an agreement on the proposed Taft-Hartley changes; Vice President Nixon said you didn't, and it was all apparently a misunderstanding. Could we have your version on that conflict?
>
> *President Eisenhower:* I will not give you a version on that conflict because, as you people know, I have consistently refused ever to speak of a personality publicly. It is not my business as President. I will say this: to my knowledge, I have never broken an agreement with an associate of mine in my life. If I have ever broken an agreement, it was something that I did not understand was made. Now, I have never broken one that I know of. And if there is anyone here who has contrary evidence, he can have the floor and make his speech (Public Papers of the Presidents, 1960, page 624).

The reader will note the many *negatives* (not, never), the frequent use of *adverbial intensifiers* (consistently, ever), and the repeated use of the personal pronoun *I.*

The Grammar of Planned Deception (Alibis). Is there any pattern of verbal behavior associated with planned deception or the telling of an alibi? Here the liar has had time to create a plausible story and to present it in a way that may fool the listener.

The principal goal of planned deception is to avoid arousing the suspicion of the intended victim. Many people apparently believe that liars are evasive, do not look directly at their victims, and tend to squirm when speaking. Clever con artists are familiar with this stereotype and tailor their behavior to create an opposite impression (Hocking & Leathers, 1980). They may approach their victims with an air of studied calm.

But what about the prepared liar's choice of grammatical structures? As we have previously noted, speakers have little conscious control of the manner in which they put words together to form sentences. Is it possible that prepared liars betray themselves by their verbal behavior? If we assume that prepared deception will have the same effect on grammatical choices as other kinds of prepared verbal acts, our categories may be of some help in detecting alibis.

We know from our study of spontaneity in speech that the more carefully remarks are crafted, the fewer qualifying phrases they contain. From this discovery, it is only a short step to the assumption that prepared liars can be expected to show less spontaneity in their spoken remarks. According to our hypothesis, they will use fewer qualifying phrases when telling their alibis than when speaking the truth.

Spontaneity and Law Enforcement

Experienced criminals create alibis in order to avoid giving themselves away in unstructured police investigations. A colleague who works in the area of forensic psychiatry has suggested the following uses of verbal analysis in police work. A verbatim transcript of an arrested suspect's first remarks to the police would permit an accurate measurement of the frequency of occurrence of qualifying phrases. It would then be possible to determine whether we are dealing with spontaneous remarks or an alibi. In other cases, it may be necessary to determine the authenticity of transcribed statements when the putative source is no longer available. Measuring the frequency of *qualifiers* could help determine whether or not the remarks were spontaneous and, therefore, authentic or, if too fluent, possibly altered by transcription.

The Verbal Behavior of Sociopaths in Unstructured Situations

Myron Eichler, a former colleague of mine at the University of Maryland, applied my method of verbal behavior analysis to the extemporaneous speech samples of a group of sociopathic men imprisoned at the Patuxent Institute, Maryland's psychiatric penitentiary. One of Eichler's findings was that compared to normal control subjects, the sociopaths used significantly more *qualifiers*. Of all the deviant groups tested by my method, the sociopaths were the only ones to use significantly more qualifying phrases than normal controls. How can we explain this finding? One possible explanation is that individuals who tend to get into compromising situations are extremely careful about making verbal commitments. They require time to construct plausible stories to account for their behavior. Since Eichler did not give them time to prepare their monologues, the Patuxent sociopaths displayed great caution in their spontaneous remarks, a phenomenon reflected by a high density of *qualifiers* (Eichler, 1966).

Spontaneity in the Courtroom

Preparation of witnesses for sworn testimony in court is an important part of a lawyer's success in trial work. To be convincing, a witness should be categorical. "*I think* the defendant was the man who pulled the trigger" is not persuasive testimony. If surprised by too many questions on cross-examination, the witness may appear to be unsure of the testimony. A good trial attorney can usually anticipate most of the difficult questions the opposing attorney will raise and review them with the client before cross-examination. Surprise rather than confrontation is the trial lawyer's most potent weapon. It forces the witness to retrieve and encode memories from his or her lexicon. The resulting hesitation and qualification will make the testimony appear less credible to a jury.

Lie Detection: Some Concluding Remarks

So we terminate our discussion of deception on a somewhat disappointing note. We have failed, as have our predecessors, to find a magic key that will enable us to detect lying by means of verbal analysis. What is even more discouraging is the realization that the problem cannot be easily solved by more refined methods. Whether we approach the problem of lie detection through verbal or nonverbal methods, we encounter obstacles having to do with the complexity of human recall and the personal nature of truth.

THE GRAMMAR OF DECISION

In considering the increased applications of the category, *qualifiers*, the reader will have noticed the occasional association I have made between its use and the personality trait of indecisiveness. Few character traits are more important than the ability to decide, to reconsider, and to stick to a decision if it is in one's interests to do so. How is decision making reflected by our grammatical choices?

Analyzing Decision Making

It is useful, I believe, to divide the process of decision making into three components: (1) preparation, (2) decision, and (3) reconsideration. Simple observation suggests that one or more of these steps may be pathologically affected in a given individual.

Once the context of a speaker's remarks is known, it is possible to estimate the amount of qualification to expect. The reader need only refer to Chapter 2, page 28, to learn the approximate use of qualifying phrases in a number of speaking situations. If, in a given case, the frequency of occurrence of *qualifiers* exceeds one's expectations, it is likely that the speaker may be having difficulty preparing a course of action.

Once a course of action has been chosen, it is time for implementation. Again, observation suggests that the use of the indicative mood with the personal pronoun *I* as the subject of action verbs (or the "imperial we" in the case of leaders), best reflects the ability to take action and to accept responsibility for it. Excessive use of passive constructions, particularly the passive without agent ("It was done in an awkward manner") suggests a problem in executing previously planned actions.

Finally, there is reconsideration of action already taken. The category *retractors* appears to reflect this cognitive function. I consider a dearth of *retractors* to indicate inadequate reconsideration, a single-minded, dogmatic approach to the resolution of problems.

But what about an excessive use of retractors? Here we are on firmer ground. If combined with a moderate use of *qualifiers*, a high frequency of occurrence of *retractors* suggests impulsivity. Why? Because inadequately prepared decisions often have to be reversed. A group of impulsive patients I tested a number of years ago, did, in fact, use significantly more *retractors* than a group of normal control subjects (Weintraub & Aronson, 1964). So did a group of female binge-eaters, women who could not control the urge to consume enormous quantities of food. The binge-eaters' eating episodes were apparently brought on by periods of loneliness and were succeeded by feelings of guilt and attempts to undo the effects of the overeating (Weintraub & Aronson, 1969).

How should we interpret low scores in both *qualifiers* and *retractors* categories? In my judgment, such a pattern indicates quickness in making decisions and an ability to stick to them. Assuming that the speaker's remarks have not been planned, that these remarks are truly spontaneous, we might have a person who is quick and discerning or quick and foolish, depending upon the degree of wisdom demonstrated.

Paralysis of Decision

Very high scores in both *qualifiers* and *retractors* categories reflects the pattern of the classical obsessive-compulsive individual. Such persons tend to decide slowly, fear they have made mistakes, reconsider, decide again, reconsider, and so on ad infinitum. The impact on the listener is that of a speaker who is paralyzed with indecision.

In assessing a speaker's ability to decide wisely, I prefer to see moderate amounts of qualifying and retracting. Such a pattern indicates that the speaker is carefully considering the alternatives before deciding, and reconsidering, if necessary, before taking definitive action. All this without wasting too much time in the process.

The Pathology of Decision Making:
Some Clinical Examples

We have described some of the verbal reflections of decision-making problems. How do they manifest themselves in everyday clinical work? Let us consider some of the more common varieties.

The Impulsive Patient. Impulsive people usually have normal qualifying scores and high frequencies of *retractors*. Their symptomatic behavior is characterized by foolish decisions and attempts, generally unsuccessful, to undo the effects of their impulsivity. The following excerpt from the monologue of a young, male college student, admitted to a university psychiatric inpatient service for suicidal behavior, illustrates the verbal behavior of an impulsive patient:

> I am interested in some sports, mainly wrestling, football, *although* I'm not big enough to play football, considering I'm 5'7½" and weigh about 150 pounds. *But* in wrestling, I think I could do well. I've wrestled in school some and the college doesn't have a team right now, *but* I'm trying to work on them to get a team in the near future, *although* I'm not going back this semester. I'd like to go back part-time next semester, the fall semester. I'd be working and going part-time. It would take a bit longer, *but* I think it would work out much better, it'd be a step to the future.

The reader will note the many *retractors*, which I've italicized. This patient's use of *retractors* was approximately three times that of normal male volunteers. His use of *qualifiers* was within normal limits.

A *Patient Paralyzed by Indecision*. The following excerpt is from a free-speech monologue recorded by a female patient admitted to a university inpatient unit for mixed depressive and compulsive symptoms. Incapacitated by a number of compulsive rituals, she had difficulty making the most routine decisions. The "hemming and hawing" quality of her speech strongly reflects her paralysis of decision. Note the numerous *qualifiers* and *retractors*, which suggest problems in all phases of the decision-making process:

> I don't know what kind of a job I want or what kind of a future there is for me. *I don't think* it's hopeless or anything *but* it's sort of nebulous. I get very discouraged about that. If I had a specific job that I wanted, it wouldn't be as hard. *But* I was a secretary before. And I just don't want to be that way anymore. I want something that's more rewarding—not financially *but* just to me. *I think* this place is a very good place. They don't force you to do things like I thought they would. *Some people do.* They try to *but* they get no place with me. If I can do something on my own, I feel a lot better than if somebody forces me to do it. *But* a lot of times people just have to push me to do it or else I just wouldn't do it. *I guess* I need their approval to know that they want to do this thing. And that I should do it. And *I guess* I'm looking for somebody to guide me or—I just don't know what to do myself.

This patient's scores indicate more than twice the number of *qualifiers* and *retractors* than the average speaker. This excerpt from her monologue reflects paralysis of decision in both its thematic content and grammatical choices.

Putting Things Together the Delusional Way. I want to complete this brief survey of the pathology of decision making by presenting an excerpt from the monologue of a paranoid inpatient. Although most delusional patients are cautious and have a fairly high frequency of *retractors*, there are important exceptions. Some paranoid individuals—the more dangerous ones—struggle to find an explanation for disturbing phenomena and, once having found it, no longer question their conclusions. If their delusional systems involve "enemies," violence may result. In the following free-speech sample, the reader will note the painful groping for an explanation to a "problem." The quoted remarks are full of *qualifiers* but have no *retractors*, suggesting that once an "answer" to the "problem" is found, there may be no turning back. Not long after this patient was discharged from the hospital, he murdered his wife.

I now find myself with a definite problem which I wish I could find the answer to. And *there doesn't seem* to be any definite answer within myself. The problem within me is something that I do not completely understand—whether or not it's myself or the real thing. I keep playing with the idea that *maybe* that's the trouble. *Maybe* I should distract my mind and get my mind on interests of something else of another nature, that *I may* be able to completely get the thought out of my mind. *I think, maybe,* if I go back to my art work and concentrate on different phases of learning it, that *maybe* I can renew my interests and alleviate the problem from my mind— do everything I can to cooperate with anyone I can that *might* be able to help me with this problem. And that the thing *may* find an answer for itself.

SUMMARY

In this chapter, we have continued to study the use of *qualifiers*, alone or in combination with *retractors*, in the areas of deception and decision making. What appeared to be a useless category has turned out to have practical applications in unexpected places. Although there are undoubtedly still other uses for *qualifiers*, we are ready to move on to another topic, one that has engaged the attention of students of verbal behavior much more than spontaneity— the verbal expression of emotion. In this area, as in the study of spontaneity in speech, I shall be able to present to the reader the results of some interesting experiments that will advance our understanding of the subject.

CHAPTER 4

Saying It with Feeling

Shortly after the publication of *Verbal Behavior*, the science editor of a large metropolitan newspaper was preparing a feature story on my research. During one of our phone conversations, she announced that she had solved a problem that had been bothering her for a long time. It concerned one of her newspaper colleagues. Jack, a middle-aged journalist, was considered to be a kind and generous person by those who knew him well. Yet he had a cold, detached way of speaking. She had often wondered what it was about Jack's speech that conveyed this impression of aloofness. After studying my verbal categories, she had come to the conclusion that he used few, if any, "expressions of feelings." This verbal mannerism, she was convinced, was responsible for the cold, dry quality of his speech. Was she correct? This chapter will attempt to answer the question raised by the science editor. What *are* the verbal reflections of emotion in speech?

VERBAL VERSUS NONVERBAL
REFLECTIONS OF EMOTION

It may come as a surprise to the reader to learn that identifying those speech variables associated with the expression of feeling has been one of the most difficult and controversial tasks for students of communication. Many researchers scoff at the very notion that emotion can be expressed by mere words. These investigators look primarily to nonverbal behavior for reflections of feelings in speech. And there is some experimental evidence to support their position. I have reviewed this evidence in some detail in *Verbal Behavior*. Let me briefly summarize the arguments of the "nonverbal" investigators or paralinguists.

49

Those who believe that nonverbal speech signals, such as vocalizations, hesitations, and incomplete sentences, are the principal conveyors of emotion present the following arguments: (1) Important emotional exchanges obviously occur between mother and child during the preverbal stages of child development. Is it not logical to assume that the gestures, facial expressions, and vocalizations that transmit these emotional messages continue to be the most important means of affective expression throughout life (Moskowitz, 1978)? (2) Certain investigators working with congenitally hearing-impaired children raised by hearing-impaired parents have reported that such children can grow into perfectly well-adjusted adults. They have no more emotional problems than children with normal speech and hearing. Such an outcome would be most unlikely without continuous and significant exchanges of feelings between parent and child (Vernon & Miller, 1973). (3) Researchers have published studies showing that filtered, content-free speech—that is, speech that has been purged of understandable words, leaving only nonverbal sounds—can communicate to listeners certain emotions by means of such voice qualities as pitch, tone, volume, rate, and rhythm (Milmoe, Rosenthal, Blane, Chafetz, and Wolf, 1967). Do not such reports offer impressive evidence against the importance of verbal language for the expression of emotion?

In the face of these powerful and persuasive arguments, we students of verbal behavior are tempted to give up the fight and agree with our paralinguistic colleagues that words are indeed unimportant in expressing feelings. There are, however, certain facts that the paralinguists' arguments do not take into account.

It is true, for example, that the preverbal infant can have emotional exchanges with its parent. This does not mean, however, that words play no part in these exchanges. Long before they begin to speak intelligibly, children appear to be familiar with the rhythm and intonational contours of their parents' language. Although adults' words may not be understood as verbal signals, they undoubtedly play a role in molding these contours, which help shape future grammatical development. We know that children, by making sounds with certain stress and intonational patterns, can produce declarative, interrogative, and imperative sentences before they can utter recognizable words. When listening to an infant's babbling from a distance, we sometimes have the odd feeling that he or she is speaking intelligible sentences. In a sense, the infant can already understand and speak the adult language of its society before it knows the meaning of a single word (Menyuk, 1969).

Assertions that congenitally hearing-impaired children raised by hearing-impaired parents may develop free of extensive emotional illness have been challenged by certain investigators (Edelheit, 1969). Even if these assertions were true, however, it does not follow that the role of verbal speech is unimportant in the socialization of children with normal hearing. Would anyone contend that hands are not important for writing because people without them can be taught to write with their feet?

Those who belittle the importance of words in the expression of feelings seem to forget that poems, novels, and plays have been stirring human emotions for thousands of years. Who would bother to write a love letter or a suicide note if words could not arouse the emotions of a reader?

Once we have accepted the possibility that words may be important conveyors of emotions, we still have the problem of investigating the extent to which the feelings expressed are reflections of the meaning or the formal arrangement of the words. I have always believed that both semantic and syntactic aspects of written and spoken language are able to evoke feelings in listeners and readers.

CONVEYING FEELINGS THROUGH MEANING OR GRAMMATICAL CHOICE

Intuitively, most of us would agree that emotion can reside in the meanings of words. Consider the following two sentences:

1. John's knife pierced his artichoke's heart.
2. John's knife pierced his mother's heart.

The two sentences are grammatically identical. Yet to most people, sentence two communicates a higher intensity of feeling. The reason must lie in the act of murder, particularly the horror of matricide. No matter how dramatically phrased, the gastronomical destruction of a vegetable will not have the same impact on a reader or listener.

That meaning can convey emotion seems so apparent that it is hardly worth the effort to investigate the proposition in a systematic way. Transmission of emotion by means of grammatical choice is quite another matter. If feelings are, indeed, conveyed by the formal arrangement of words, it is a far less obvious proposition and one that does require proof.

To date, investigators have been unable to identify those syntactic variables that are most important in transmitting feelings. There are formidable procedural obstacles complicating the study of emotions in the laboratory. Feelings are difficult to provoke and to sustain. They have also frustrated efforts at precise measurement.

Most researchers who have studied the transmission of emotion have focused on particular feelings, such as fear and anger. This line of research has faced two major methodological problems: (1) How can a feeling be defined so that independent judges can agree among themselves on its outward manifestations? (2) How can experimental subjects be made to experience and to transmit emotions over a long enough period of time so that the various speech characteristics chosen for study can be measured? The following are some of the strategies developed by communication researchers.

One common strategy is to ask volunteers to convey, under experimental conditions, a suggested emotion. Other subjects, acting as judges, attempt to determine the quality of the feeling expressed. Certain investigators have used hypnosis to suggest specific feelings. Others have employed paid actors (Fairbanks & Hoaglin, 1941; Feldstein, 1964).

In order to provoke more genuine feelings, experimental subjects have been placed in anxiety-stimulating situations, such as stress interviews, or in anger provoking situations where they have been subjected to various frustrations or actual physical punishment. Certain researchers have had their subjects view "emotional films" or read provocative articles in attempts to arouse specific emotions.

How can feelings be studied in more natural, less contrived ways? If we are willing to sacrifice experimental rigor, we can sample natural conversations, psychotherapy sessions, initial psychiatric interviews, and so on. Another method is to try to identify individuals who are predisposed to the expression of certain feelings by administering screening tests to a large number of volunteers and then selecting those who score highest for the presence of those feelings we wish to study. We assume, for example, that a group of volunteers who score high on an anxiety scale will reflect their anxious dispositions in their speech. The chosen subjects' verbal behavior can then be sampled in a variety of natural settings.

Even if independent judges agree on the outward manifestations of a certain feeling, we can never be certain that the perceived emotion is what the experimental subject is actually feeling. In our present state of knowledge, we cannot measure with more assurance something as transient as a feeling. Researchers have been content to accept the verdict of naive judges as to the genuineness of a feeling they are asked to identify or measure.

MEASURING EMOTIONAL EXPRESSION

In this chapter, we shall begin the study of emotion in speech by considering its expression as a single variable. Rather than investigating particular feelings such as anger, love, and fear, we shall focus on the *intensity* of expressed emotion. The intensity of emotional expression is far from being a trivial matter in the behavioral sciences. For centuries, physicians have observed that certain schizophrenic patients do not express the same range and intensity of emotion as normal individuals. It is common for psychiatrists to refer to the kind of affective expression seen in schizophrenia as "flat." But what exactly *is* flat affect? Does the "flatness" reside entirely in the gestures, facial expressions, and vocal dynamics? Do word choices play a part, and, if so, is it primarily choice of vocabulary or is it the formal arrangement of the words that contributes to the effect? There have been some attempts to associate the intensity of emotional expression with choice of grammatical structures, but no agreed-upon style has been identified.

I decided to approach the problem of measuring the intensity of emotion in speech in the following way. Of my verbal categories, I assumed that *nonpersonal references* would best measure the amount of feeling expressed in a sample of speech. *Nonpersonal references* tend to convey an impression of detachment and aloofness that should detract from the emotional impact of a message. I believed that the higher the percentage of nonpersonal references, the lower the intensity of expressed emotion. I further assumed that the use of two other categories would be positively associated with emotional intensity: *expressions of feeling* and *direct references*, the latter category because its use implies an attempt by the speaker to engage the listener directly.

Since I was interested only in the verbal aspects of emotional expression, it was important to eliminate from the study all traces of nonverbal communication. But how?

Preparing Messages Free of Nonverbal Cues

I chose samples of about 250 words from the typed transcripts of 10 normal male subjects. These samples had been gathered from men serving in the United States Armed Forces during the mid-1950s. They had volunteered to serve as subjects for certain experiments sponsored by the U.S. Army and, as part of their psychological evaluation, were asked to speak into a tape recorder for 10 minutes on any subject or subjects they wished. The tapes were transcribed and have been used in a number of verbal studies. For the present experiment, typed transcripts of the first 250 words of each of 10 monologues were given to 11 first-year medical students enrolled in an elective psychiatry course at the University of Maryland. The students were asked to read the protocols and to rank-order them according to the "amount of feeling expressed." The students were told to ignore the quality of feeling and to rank the transcripts according to the intensity of emotion expressed. Only complete words were included in the transcripts. No partial words, signs of hesitation, or punctuation marks suggesting emotion, such as exclamation points, appeared in the transcripts.

When the rankings of the students were compared, there was significant agreement among them with respect to the intensity of emotion perceived[1]. Since all paralinguistic cues had been eliminated, this agreement was solely on the basis of verbal stimulation.

I then looked to see if any of my verbal categories distinguished the "high feelings" transcripts from the "low feelings" protocols. Two categories, *qualifiers* and *evaluators*, were positively associated with the expression of emotion. Of the three categories I predicted would separate the high from the low-feelings protocols, none, in fact, did. How can we account for the unexpected results?

I reasoned that it was likely that two factors led to the rejection of my hypotheses. One had to do with the thematic content of the transcripts, which, in certain cases, may have communicated strong emotion to the judges. One speaker, for example, used few *expressions of feeling*, many *nonpersonal references*, and no direct references. Yet he was judged to communicate a high intensity of emotion. Why? Let us look at a paragraph from his transcript, which was concerned with highway safety, a seemingly bland subject:

> But so many individuals will jump into a strange car without familiarizing himself with it, strike up down the road and first thing you know he is actually in a strange vehicle, a good driver who has got himself into the position—beyond the point of no—of escape and the accident's there . . . . Now, when we think of the 40,000 lives approximately that has been

---

[1] $\rho sb = 0.92$. Internal consistency reliability, based on a split half reliability coefficient followed by application of the Spearman Brown formula (Guilford, 1965).

lost each year in our own United States here, to say nothing of the hundreds or so thousands of permanent injuries . . .

The reader will note the speaker's use of certain expressions like "jump into a strange car," "strike up down the road," and "thousands of permanent injuries." It is possible that in the case of this speaker, the *meaning* of the words carried a more powerful emotional message than their formal arrangement. There is, however, another possibility. Certain of the volunteers may have been transmitting feeling by means of grammatical structures not yet included in my system.

Let us compare our highway safety speaker with one who chose to talk on the subject of military government, an equally unexciting topic. This speaker made a similarly sparse use of my "feelings" categories and was judged by the students to convey very little emotion:

A platoon is the basic unit of the military government unit, consisting of three officers, five enlisted men. The functions of a platoon commander and assistants: The platoon, senior noncommissioned officer, platoon sergeant, assisted by a public safety sergeant, special investigator, clerk typist, and a clerk. The public safety sergeant is responsible for control of the police department, fire department, department of welfare.

Our "military government" speaker certainly chose a subject less apt to arouse fantasies of death and mutilation in the minds of the judges. But before concluding that only differences in meaning accounted for the judges' reactions to the two transcripts, let us see if previously unmeasured grammatical structures may have been responsible, in part, for the rankings.

New "Feelings" Categories

In order further to investigate the impact of grammatical choice on transmission of emotion, I designed an experiment that tested the emotional impact of new grammatical categories, while neutralizing the effects of thematic content. After considerable thought and a review of the literature, I chose the following 13 categories as most likely to be involved in the communication of feeling. Seven of the 13 categories were among those I was already using and are, therefore, familiar to the reader. They are: (1) *nonpersonal references,* (2) *expressions of feeling,* (3) *direct references,* (4) *evaluators,* (5) *qualifiers,* (6) *I/we ratio,* and (7) *negatives.* The reader will note that the first three categories were those I incorrectly predicted would distinguish the "high feelings" from the "low feelings" protocols. *Evaluators* and *qualifiers* were the two categories that *did* significantly distinguish the high from the low emotion transcripts. I included the *I/we ratio* believing that the personal "I" would convey more feeling to a listener or reader than "we." Since they often reflect oppositional behavior, I assumed that *negatives* would convey more feeling than positive remarks.

The six new categories were all developed from grammatical structures. They are the following:

1. *Active versus passive voice.* I assumed that the active voice would be perceived as more forceful and, therefore, as conveying more emotion ("John *threw* the ball" versus "The ball was thrown by John").

2. I believed that *contractions* would increase the emotional impact of a message ("I *won't* resign from office" versus "I *will not* resign from office").

3. Since speakers sometimes shift from the past to the historical present in order to dramatize a story, I reasoned that the *present* tense conveys more feeling than the *past* tense ("The bear *is approaching* me and I'm *getting* very nervous" versus "The bear *approached* me and I *was getting* very nervous").

4. I predicted that *commands* would convey more feeling than the ordinary indicative mood ("Close the door!" versus "You are closing the door").

5. Since rhetorical questions are consciously used by speakers to arouse listeners' feelings, I believed that they would increase the emotional intensity of a message ("Is there no hope for us?" versus "There is no hope for us").

6. *Adverbial intensifiers* have been described as expressions that increase the dramatic force of a statement. I reasoned that they would also be perceived by listeners as adding to the amount of feeling conveyed by a speaker's remark ("I want that car" versus "I *really* want that car").

EXPERIMENT II: THE GRAMMATICAL EXPRESSION OF EMOTION

Having prepared my "feelings" categories, I proceeded to test which, if any, of the 13 were judged by readers to add to the emotional force of a message. It was first necessary to eliminate thematic content as a confounding variable. I constructed a questionnaire consisting of 130 pairs of sentences, 10 for each of the 13 categories. Each pair of sentences dealt with the same subject matter and differed only in the grammatical category for which I was testing. The items representing the 13 categories were presented in a random manner to 10 medical students, six men and four women. The students were asked to indicate for each of the 130 pairs of sentences which of the two expressed the greater amount of feeling. The following 13 pairs of sentences, one for each category, have been taken from the actual questionnaire used in the experiment. They will give the reader an idea of how the items were constructed. In each case, the grammatical structure being tested for has been italicized.

1. *Qualifiers.*
   a. I *believe* that justice will triumph in the end.
   b. Justice will triumph in the end.

2. *Adverbial Intensifiers.*
   a. He *absolutely* refuses to go.
   b. He refuses to go.

3. *I versus we.*
   a. *I* have never compromised with evil.
   b. *We* have never compromised with evil

4. *Contractions.*
   a. I *didn't* stop at the red light.
   b. I did not stop at the red light.

5. *Direct References.*
   a. Do *you* have the time?
   b. Does somebody have the time?

6. *Negatives.*
   a. He has *no* chance to win the lottery.
   b. He has a chance to win the lottery.

7. *Present tense.*
   a. Mr. Thompson *is* working in the yard.
   b. Mr. Thompson was working in the yard.

8. *Rhetorical Question.*
   a. *Do we not* deserve better?
   b. We do not deserve better.

9. *Expressions of feeling.*
   a. Jimmy *pleased* me again.
   b. Jimmy visited me again.

10. *Active voice.*
    a. Dan *will win* the race.
    b. The race will be won by Dan.

11. *Evaluators.*
    a. He gave an *excellent* performance last night.
    b. He have a two-hour performance last night.

12. *Personal References.*
    a. *Georgette* baked a delicious cake.
    b. She baked a delicious cake.

13. *Commands.*
    a. *Wipe that grin* off your face.
    b. You are wiping that grin off your face.

No nonverbal indications of emotion were included in the questionnaire, such as exclamation points, incomplete, or repeated words. The student–judges were asked to complete the questionnaire items quickly and intuitively. All judges finished the task within half an hour.

In order to evaluate the degree to which the raters confirmed my hypotheses, the proportion of congruent responses was compared with a chance outcome (.50) by means of a t-test for proportions. The results for each category are shown in Table 4.1.

Eight of 13 hypotheses were confirmed. The following categories were considered by the judges to convey emotion: (1) The use of *I* rather than *we*, (2) *Adverbial intensifiers*, (3) *Direct references*, (4) *Expressions of feeling*, (5) The *active mood*, (6) *personal references*, (7) *commands*, and (8) *evaluators*. The results of Experiment II clearly indicate that grammatical structures can convey emotion after we have controlled for thematic content and paralinguistic clues.

The reader will note that *qualifiers*, which significantly distinguished "high feelings" from "low feelings" protocols in the first experiment, failed to do so in Experiment II. Why? The most reasonable explanation is that while *qualifiers* do not themselves convey feeling, they may be associated with grammatical structures that do. We have already noted in Chapter 2 that *qualifiers* serve as a marker for spontaneity in speech. It is likely that planned speech is

TABLE 4.1 Proportion of Judges' Ratings of Expressed Emotion Congruent with Author's Predictions

Category	Proportion	t	p <
I/we	.88	8.14	.001
Contractions	.54	0.36	—
Expressions of feeling	.94	10.99	.001
Direct references	.79	4.53	.01
Qualifiers	.36	−1.33	—
Rhetorical questions	.65	1.96	—
Commands	.87	11.05	.001
Adverbial intensifiers	.78	4.58	.01
Present/past	.65	1.83	—
Evaluators	.93	16.52	.001
Personal references	.72	3.02	.02
Active/passive	.72	3.09	.02
Positive/negative	.49	−0.12	—

In all cases, df = 9.

less expressive than extemporaneous or impromptu speech. Previous research findings show that the frequency of occurrence of qualifying phrases parallels that of evaluators, which were judged in both experiments to convey feeling (Weintraub & Aronson, 1962). Qualifying phrases often contain the pronoun, I, which was perceived by the student–judges to be more expressive than *we*. The results of Experiment II demonstrate that when *qualifiers* cannot "piggyback" on other grammatical structures, they no longer convey emotion.

The fact that a category in Experiment II was judged to convey emotion does not necessarily mean that it does so, to an important degree, in ordinary conversations. Certain of the categories are not used very frequently by many speakers. Commands and the passive voice, for example, are used sparingly by many people. In any case, they do not occur often enough in free speech monologues to be treated statistically.

It is likely that different speakers express emotion by using different grammatical structures. In reviewing the protocols used in Experiment I, I was able to ascertain that not all speakers used the same devices in conveying feeling. Most "emotional" speakers used few *nonpersonal references*, a high I/we ratio, and a fair number of *expressions of feeling*. There were, however, some interesting exceptions. One speaker, for example, who was judged to be an expressive speaker, used almost no *expressions of feeling* and many *nonpersonal references*. He also made little use of the pronoun I. Of all the transcripts, however, his contained the highest number of *evaluators* and *adverbial intensifiers*.

A New Category—Adverbial Intensifiers

In order to study the grammatical expression of emotion, we have created several new categories. One of them, *adverbial intensifiers*, appears to reflect extremely important personality characteristics. Since its frequency of occurrence in most speaking situations allows for statistical analysis, I decided to test its usefulness as a regular category in my verbal analysis system.

In the psycholinguistic literature, *adverbial intensifiers* have often been associated with histrionic behavior ("Charlotte is *so* beautiful!" or "Jack is a *very* interesting young man") (Key, 1975). People who exaggerate, who see the world in black and white terms, who like to dramatize events, supposedly use more adverbial intensifiers than less flamboyant speakers. But do they? Most reports linking adverbial intensifiers to dramatic behavior have been anecdotal in nature. Would a rigorous study of the uses of adverbial intensifiers confirm these anecdotal reports?

The Use of Adverbial Intensifiers by Normal Speakers. Since the frequency of adverbial intensifiers has been reported to vary with age and sex, I decided to measure its use in the speech of normal speakers from early childhood to old age, comparing males and females at each age level. The subjects were divided into the following six age groups: 5–7, 9–11, 12–14, 15–17, 18–45, and 60–85. The groups were composed of approximately equal numbers of males and females (Table 4.2). The four groups under the age of 18 were recruited from a private, coeducational school in the Baltimore area. The young adult group consisted of male volunteers from the armed forces and female hospital employees. The 60–85-year-old subjects were recruited from the Waxter Center for Senior Citizens, operated by the City of Baltimore. All subjects were active, alert, of normal intelligence, and relatively free of crippling physical and psychological disorders [2].

Ten-minute free-speech monologues were obtained from subjects in all age groups. The speech samples were transcribed and scored for adverbial intensifiers. A two-way factorial analysis of variance was performed for age and sex. Significant differences were found for both age ($F = 10.68$, df $= 5$, $p < .01$) and sex ($F = 23.68$, df $= 1$, $p < .01$). A Newman-Keuls test revealed that the midadolescents

TABLE 4.2 Number of Subjects in Each Age Group in Statistical Analyses

Group	Age	Males	Females
Early schoolers	5–7	7	4
Latency children	9–11	8	9
Young adolescents	12–14	10	10
Midadolescents	15–17	8	8
Adults	18–45	23	23
Senior citizens	60–85	10	10

[2] With the exception of the young adult group, 10 male and 10 female subjects were recruited for all age groups. Almost all subjects in the various age groups, with the exception of the youngest, were able to follow the data-collection procedure and to provide the required minimum of 200 words. Of the 20 children in the 5–7-year-old age group, only 11 spoke enough to be included in the study. In several instances, we were unable to transcribe tapes of subjects in the older age groups because of technical difficulties.

used significantly more adverbial intensifiers than all other age groups. The early schoolers were significantly lower than the other groups. The mean values and standard errors of means are shown in Figure 4.1.

For males, the highest *adverbial intensifiers* scores occurred in the latency (9–11) and midadolescent (15–17) age groups. The age differences for the males were modest. This was not the case for the female volunteers. After obtaining rather low scores in the 5–7 and 9–11 age groups (somewhat below the male subjects), the female speakers showed an explosive increase in the use of adverbial intensifiers during adolescence and young adulthood, significantly exceeding the male subjects in those age periods. Interestingly, the sex differences disappeared in old age when the males had a slight but nonsignificant advantage. Another noteworthy finding is that both male and female "early schoolers" had the lowest scores of all the groups.

What sense can we make of these data? One explanation seems to account for most of the findings. The age and sex differences seem to be almost entirely due to high frequencies of occurrence among females in the "courtship" age groups, adolescence and young adulthood. *Adverbial intensifiers*, when used in great numbers, tend to contribute to a dramatic presentation characteristic of young women (Key, 1975). This may be an example of sexual behavior which, according to Birdwhistell, young female children mature into and older women give up (Birdwhistell, 1974).

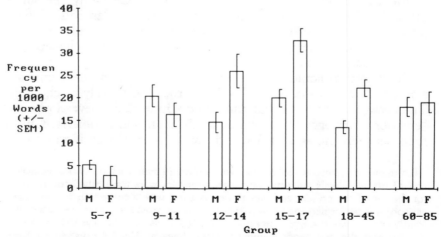

FIGURE 4.1 Use of adverbial intensifiers as a function of age and sex.

The finding that adolescent and adult females significantly exceed males in the use of adverbial intensifiers helps resolve a problem raised in my book, *Verbal Behavior*. Unlike a number of other investigators, I could find no difference between males and females in the *expressions of feeling* category. I wrongly assumed that this category would adequately reflect verbal emotion in ordinary conversations. The results of our experiments clearly indicate a *variety* of grammatical expressions of feeling. While men and women do not differ in all "expressive" categories, they do in several of them. In addition to *adverbial intensifiers*, women use significantly more *evaluators* than men (Aronson & Weintraub, 1967a). They also use the present tense more and the past tense less than male speakers[3].

Greater use of these three categories gives female speech a "here and now," colorful flavor that is more likely to be perceived by listeners and readers as "emotional."

Verbal Expression of Emotion in Children and Adolescents

What is it about the speech of small children that strikes the listener as uninhibited and expressive? The reader will recall that in Chapter 2 we could not discover significantly greater grammatical reflections of spontaneity in children's speech when compared to that of adults. We attributed its freshness and unpredictability to thematic content and paralinguistic devices. Certainly, the simple and naive themes in children's speech provide elements of surprise and delight to the adult ear. The meanings that children give to certain words are quite idiosyncratic and add to the element of surprise (Laffal, 1965).

Compared to adults, do children use more "emotional" expressions, and, if they do, which kinds are they most likely to choose? The answer seems to be that children do, indeed, use several of our "emotional" categories more frequently than adult subjects. Children between the ages of five and seven use significantly more *I*'s,

---

[3] Ten-minute free-speech monologues were collected from each of 23 normal male and 23 normal female subjects. The speech samples were transcribed and scored for the use of the present and past tenses. A t-test with a correction for unequal variance was performed and showed that the women used the present tense significantly more than the males (means: 62.2 ± 3.8 vs. 45.1 ± 4.0; $t = 3.11$; $df = 44$; $p < .01$) and the past tense significantly less (means: 31.4 ± 4.2 vs. 46.7 ± 4.2; $t = 2.56$; $df = 44$; $p < .05$).

expressions of feeling, and fewer *nonpersonal references* when asked to provide 10 minutes of free, uninterrupted speech (Weintraub, 1981). As I've already indicated above, small children use fewer *adverbial intensifiers* than adults, probably because of the grammatical complexity of this category. In *Verbal Behavior,* I gave the following two examples of rather unrestrained verbal expression recorded by two six-year-old boys. (Girls in this age group tended to be shy, less expressive, and more socially appropriate than the boys.)

FIRST BOY: Shut up you monkey. . . . Get out before I hit you. . . . This has been a recording of your silly recording. . . . So long folks, this has been a recording of your silly quack quack.

SECOND BOY: Get out of here or I'll karate your rear end off. . . . Good-bye, dodo brain. See you all later. So long, alligator, in a while crocodile. Bye-bye, rotten egg, dodo brain, dummy do-do. . . . What's up, Doc?

I wish to bring the reader's attention to the frequent use of *commands* by the two children. Among the normal subjects I have studied, only children used commands when asked to speak freely in the presence of a technician. The use of commands by adult volunteers usually indicates the presence of psychopathology, as we shall see below.

The 9-to-11-year-old or "latency" children behaved in a very calm and businesslike manner when asked to speak freely for 10 minutes. They performed their tasks efficiently and without trying to provoke or engage the technician in the room. Unlike the "early schoolers" or adolescents, there appeared to be little discomfort or passion in the verbal expression of the 9 to 11 age group. The reader will not be surprised to learn that latency-aged children did not score particularly high in any of the "emotional" categories. Children in this age group showed a remarkable decrease in the use of the pronoun, *I,* and a corresponding increase in the pronoun, *we.* This change is altogether congruent with the well-known preoccupation of latency-aged children with group activities (Weintraub, 1981).

What about the expression of emotion in adolescence? Young adolescents (aged 12–14) tended to be self-conscious and easily embarrassed when speaking publicly. Their feelings were more apt to be expressed in nonverbal ways. When asked to speak uninterruptedly for 10 minutes, the young adolescents were far less at ease than the latency children, as the following two examples demonstrate:

GIRL: I'm making an idiot out of myself. . . . I'm wrecking the tape because I have nothing to say. . . . She's (the technician) looking at
me as if I'm some kind of idiot. . . . Oh God! I hope I don't have
much more time left.

BOY: I enjoy talking, but I like to have someone answering me so it
doesn't look like I'm talking to myself, like I'm crazy.

On the whole, the early adolescents showed little grammatical expression of feeling. *Nonpersonal references*, for example, were higher
than in any other age group (Weintraub, 1981). The one exception
to this tight control of verbal expressiveness was the frequent use of
adverbial intensifiers among the girls.

Midadolescents (aged 15–17) made frequent use of certain
"expressive" categories. Compared to the adult speakers, their free
speech samples contained significantly more *expressions of feeling,
direct references*, and *evaluators*. Midadolescents also used more *adverbial intensifiers* than any other age group, young or old. Midado-
lescence is truly the age of hyperbole. The following excerpt from
the spontaneous remarks of a 17-year-old female high school student
well illustrates the histrionic quality of adolescent speech:

> Okay, I'm supposed to talk about anything I want so I'll just start talking
> about school. I'm here at _____ School right now and I just had a
> French class, one of the most boring in my life. We talked about the future
> and how some things are more future than other things, that some things
> are so close together in the future that they're not more future than other
> things even though you have to do something before you do the other one.
> The whole thing was totally confusing and absolutely nothing which isn't
> totally unusual for a French class.

Expression of Emotion in Psychopathological States

The assessment of psychiatric patients' ability to express emotion
and the manner in which they do so are important concerns of
psychiatrists and others who work with the mentally ill. Let us see
how the various groups of emotionally impaired people I have studied differ from unimpaired individuals in the way they verbally
show feeling.

In my psycholinguistic work with patient groups, I have studied
six behaviorally distinct populations: (1) *impulsives*, individuals who
share a history of extremely uncontrollable and self-destructive behavior. Their impulsive behavior led to inpatient treatment on a university psychiatric service; (2) *delusionals*, patients who expressed

in words and actions well-systematized delusions of either a persecu-
tory or grandiose nature. My group of delusional patients were also
treated on a university inpatient service; (3) *depressives*, a third university inpatient-treated group that expressed feelings of sadness,
hopelessness, helplessness, and guilt. Many patients in this group
also expressed suicidal ideas; a number of them actually tried to kill
themselves; (4) *compulsives*, a mixed inpatient and outpatient group
whose symptoms consisted of ritualistic behavior. Patients in this
group could not control the urge to act in illogical and repetitive
ways; (5) *binge eaters*, a group of women who attended a weight-
control clinic in an attempt to develop healthier eating habits. The
women in this group were not psychiatric patients and functioned at
a higher level than the individuals in the other groups; and (6) *alcoholics*, another all-female group, characterized by an alcoholic history
and inpatient status on a state hospital rehabilitation unit (Table 4.3).

How did these six groups of patients express emotion when
asked to speak freely for 10 minutes on any subject or subjects they
wished? Let us take the groups one at a time and see how each of
the patient populations scored in our "expressive" verbal categories
(Weintraub, 1981).

1. *Impulsives.* Members of this group made frequent use of the
following categories: the pronoun *I*, *direct references, expressions of
feeling,* and *adverbial intensifiers.*[4] The impulsive patient group occasionally used *commands*, an unusual verbal construction in adult

TABLE 4.3 Number of Subjects in Each Impaired
Group in Statistical Analysis

Group	Males	Females
Impulsives	5	10
Delusionals	7	9
Depressives	22	23
Compulsives	11	6
Binge eaters (obese)	0	18
Alcoholics	0	18
Controls	23	23

[4] A one-way analysis of variance was performed for the 7 groups (6 deviant
groups and normal control group) for *adverbial intensifiers.* Although significant
differences among the groups were found overall, $(F = 2.77; df = 6, 168; p < .05)$,
a Newman-Keuls test revealed no significant differences between groups when
compared two at a time.

free speech experiments. This combination of scores gives impulsive individuals an imperious, manipulative, and exaggerated style of speaking with which we are all familiar. The following excerpt from a sample of impulsive speech reflects its explosive quality well. The speaker was a young, adult female patient who had been hospitalized because of a suicide attempt.

> Turn it [the tape recorder] off! Turn it off! You know, I—will you turn that thing off? Turn it off! You might think it's crazy, but I hate to talk into these things. Let's talk about narcotics. I like narcotics. I took them for two years. And that's all I did. When I get out of here, I won't take them anymore. I'm a liar, I will. [laughs] No, honestly, I'm not going to take them anymore. When I get out of here, I want to get a job and get an apartment and live by myself. I don't want to live with anyone else. Just me! That's all. I'm not going to stay in the hospital either. I like this hospital, though, because the people are real nice to you and everything. It's ridiculous. You don't think this is very funny, do you? Well, I do. I don't have any friends. I have two friends, but even my mother hates all my friends.

The reader will note in the above impulsive speech sample the frequent use of the pronoun *I*, the many *expressions of feeling* ("I like," "I hate," "I want," and so on), the numerous *adverbial intensifiers* ("very," "just," "even," "honestly"), the many *commands*, and a number of *direct references* to the research technician.

2. *Depressives.* This group is the most unusual of the patient populations I have studied in their use of "expressive" categories. Compared to nonpsychiatric control subjects, depressed patients used significantly more of the following grammatical structures: *I, direct references, evaluators, adverbial intensifiers, expressions of feeling,* and the *present tense.* Of the six patient groups, only depressives and impulsives used *commands* and *rhetorical questions.*

It is easy to understand why categories such as *I, expressions of feeling, evaluators, direct references,* and *adverbial intensifiers,* should be frequently used by patients who are despondent, preoccupied with the enormity of their problems, and seeking support from the people around them. When asked to volunteer 10 minutes of spontaneous speech, many depressed patients found the task extremely difficult to complete. Silences were frequent, requests to terminate the experiment (sometimes made in the form of commands) were common, and rhetorical questions about the stress of the experimental procedure were raised. The following is an excerpt of depressed speech taken from a 10-minute free speech sample. The patient was a hospitalized middle-aged woman:

I don't know what to talk about. [pause] I really don't know. [pause] I don't know what to talk about. [pause] Only my leg hurts, and I wish they'd give me something for my legs. I don't know what to talk about. [pause] I don't know. [pause] I really don't know what to talk about. Only I'm sick. I wish they'd give me something for my legs. [pause] All I know—[pause] I want to go home. I wish they'd let me go home. [pause] They don't give me nothing for my legs. [pause] That's all I know of. [pause] They never give me nothing for my legs. [pause] That's all I know. [pause] I want to go home. [pause] It's cold in here. [pause] Can't you take me out of here? [pause] Wish you'd take me home. Oh my. [pause] Wish you'd take me out of here. [pause] Doctor, can't you take me out of here? [pause] Oh, I'm cold in here. [pause] Can't you take me out of here? . . .

The pleading, demanding tone of this depressed patient is reflected grammatically by the use of *expressions of feeling*, ("I want," "I wish"), the personal pronoun *I*, the attempt to manipulate the research technician through the use of *direct references* ("Can't you take me out of here?", "Oh, Doctor, please, I'm cold"), and the use of *rhetorical questions*. The reader will also note the presence of a number of *adverbial intensifiers* ("really," "only"), and *evaluators* ("awful," "bad").

Do Depressed Patients Live in the Past? My group of depressed patients used significantly more verbs in the present tense and fewer verbs in the past tense than a comparison group of normal individuals[5]. This finding is somewhat unexpected in view of

[5] Free speech monologues were collected from a group of 45 depressed patients (22 males, 23 females) and 46 normal control subjects (23 males, 23 females). The speech samples were transcribed and scored for the use of the present and past tenses. The results were as follows (per 1000 words):

	Present tense (Mean ± S.E.M.)	Past tense (Mean ± S.E.M.)
Normal Males	45.1 ± 4.0	49.7 ± 4.2
Depressed Males	60.9 ± 3.9	29.6 ± 4.5
Normal Females	62.2 ± 3.8	31.4 ± 4.2
Depressed Females	64.6 ± 4.6	28.6 ± 4.6

A 2×2 factorial analysis of variance for unequal sample sizes was performed. There were significant main effects for both pathology ($F = 6.8$; $df = 1, 87$; $p < .05$) and sex ($F = 4.8$; $df = 1, 87$; $p < .05$) for the past tense and ($F = 5.0$; $df = 1, 87$; $p < 0.5$), ($F = 6.5$; $df = 1, 87$; $p < .05$) for the present tense. Dunnett tests for simple effects (Winer, 1962, pp. 89–92) revealed significant differences only between unimpaired and depressed males. This suggests either that unimpaired females have a "depressive" speaking style or that the unimpaired males were somehow impaired in ways unknown to us. (*Source:* Winer, B. J. Statistical Principles in Experimental Design. New York, McGraw-Hill, 1962.)

the frequent statements made in the psychiatric literature suggesting that depressed patients are locked into the past. Supposedly, depressed individuals are prisoners of unresolved conflicts that prevent them from enjoying the present and projecting themselves into the future.

A close reading of the free speech samples of 45 depressed psychiatric inpatients gives no support to the contention that they are *consciously* preoccupied with past events. With few exceptions, my group of depressed patients spoke of their suffering in the *present*. Curiously, when they spoke of the future, it was often not in the hopeless manner attributed to depressed patients. Many approached future events in a totally unrealistic manner, denying the existence of problems and adopting an ostrichlike avoidant attitude.

In their 10-minute, free speech samples, most of the depressed patients were preoccupied with whatever discomfort, physical or psychological, was bothering them at the time of the experiment. Often this was the experiment itself! Speaking uninterruptedly for 10 minutes proved to be too much for half the depressed subjects, whose frequent silences prevented them from meeting the 200 word minimum required for their scores to be included in the statistical analysis. Those who did manage to speak 200 words or more often tried to elicit help from the research technician or pleaded with him to stop the experiment before the 10-minute period had expired.

The astute reader will protest that my depressed patients may have been escaping from past unresolved conflicts and future problems by *defensively* preoccupying themselves with relatively insignificant events in the present. This may be true, but the tendency of depressed patients to speak in the present has not, to my knowledge, been reported in the psycholinguistic literature.

Since becoming aware of the preference of depressed patients for the present tense, I have listened very carefully to how my depressed patients orient themselves in time when discussing their problems. Those who use their therapy time only to complain about present difficulties can be helped if required to focus occasionally on either past traumata, particularly losses, or future challenges.

3. *Compulsives.* When compulsive patients are discussed in the psycholinguistic literature, they are not usually considered to be emotional speakers. My group of compulsive patients certainly confirms this impression. Despite the fact that they were all psychiatric patients at the time of the free speech experiment, and therefore in some emotional distress, the compulsives did not significantly

exceed normal speakers in the use of any of the "expressive" categories, with the exception of the pronoun *I*.

The compulsive patients were very careful in their choice of words, explaining their actions in an even, methodical way, often balancing the thrust of one remark with an equally forceful retracting statement. These verbal habits resulted in high *retractors* and *explainers* scores and, together with infrequent use of "expressive" categories, gave the compulsives' speech a dry, monotonous flavor (Weintraub, 1981). The following excerpt from the transcript of a patient with both obsessive-compulsive personality traits and compulsive ritualistic symptoms illustrates the speaking style of this group of patients well.

> If my wife were here, I could—it wouldn't help either. [Pause] If I knew what subjects would be of interest to you, I would feel more—more at ease talking. [Pause] Well, I can tell you about our weekends together. The time we spend, mostly fishing. And this is both at the surf and on rivers—generally, big rivers. In hopes of big fish. But it doesn't always work out that way. And we spend evenings playing chess. And she beat me last night. It's the first time. Of course, the impact on her was much different than on me. She felt elated. I felt like I goofed, because it seemed that I should be improving just as she improved. But she played a good game. And I was a bit careless. I don't know if you play chess, but my philosophy on chess is that winning the game is predicated by the other man's mistakes. But if two people each played a perfect game, it would end up in a stalemate, in that the perfect offense could be countered by the perfect defense, and the man who's second, of course, would be on the defensive all the way to see whether he could get a perfect game.

In analyzing the above excerpt, the reader will note the impersonal style, the relative paucity of feeling words, and the large number of words used to convey relatively little information.

4. *Delusionals.* The verbal behavior of delusional patients resembles, in certain respects, that of compulsives. This is not surprising since the intellectual functions are particularly affected in these two disorders (Weintraub, 1981). Delusional patients are even more careful speakers than compulsives. They do not, as a rule, blurt out remarks and then retract them as certain compulsives are wont to do. Comments are carefully screened beforehand and uttered solemnly and cautiously. One of the results of this caution is that delusional patients speak fewer words than compulsives in a free speech experiment.

My group of delusional patients had low to moderate scores in *all* "expressive" categories. The category in which delusional patients most differed from the normal speakers is *explainers*. Delusional individuals apparently have the need to rationalize their unconventional ideas and behavior. The following is an excerpt from the transcript of a delusional patient that demonstrates some of the peculiarities I have just noted:

> My name is _____, from Baltimore, Maryland. [Pause] I lived in Baltimore for 10 years, Miami for 7 years, back to Baltimore for—well, since then. [Pause] This—this microphone is really an inhibiting factor. And so is your presence. [Pause] "Your" meaning the girl sitting right here. [Pause] I have wanted to be a psychologist too. But financially I couldn't stay in college. This looks like fascinating work. [Pause] So now what I want to be is a writer. [Pause] This obvious inability to communicate verbally [Pause] doesn't indicate that there's nothing on my mind. Or (that) I have nothing to say. It just indicates certain inhibitions I have to verbal communication for some reason. And, therefore, writing is necessary as an outlet. Everybody needs to communicate. In fact, I would say about at least 95% and, perhaps, 100% of emotional problems indicate some lack of communication in the individual's life. Perhaps one of the problems is the inability to convey emotions by words. And in this respect the animals might have an advantage over us, by their grunts and yells, although there may be just as much neuroses and psychoses in the animal kingdom. [Pause] I was thinking last night of the possibility of somehow electronically finding that morbid area in the neurotic or psychotic individual's brain and also focusing some kind of electronic beam into that area and erasing the morbid brain cells and [Pause] and—and, by doing that, curing the individual. And, perhaps, if the world survives, this will come about some day. Though it is kind of frightening when you think about how electronics and machines are controlling a great deal of our lives and having such an influence . . .

The young man who uttered the above remarks was diagnosed as paranoid schizophrenic and had well systematized delusions. The thematic content illustrates his sensitivity, suspiciousness, and fear of being controlled. His choice of grammatical structures is quite typical for delusional patients. He paused often, moved from the concrete to the general, often using impersonal and indirect speech mannerisms. There are very few "emotional" remarks in the excerpt.

5. *Binge-eaters and alcoholics.* These two groups of female speakers were less atypical in their choice of grammatical structures than the first four groups. "Oral" in their life-style, their scores resembled the depressive and impulsive speech patterns but were less extreme (Weintraub, 1981). This is not surprising when we consider the fact that the binge-eaters were not psychiatric patients and functioned at a much higher level than the more emotionally disturbed groups. The alcoholics were drawn from a rather heterogeneous group of patients, and, although resembling the depressives and impulsives in certain ways (frequent use of *I*, *me*, and *evaluators*), did not deviate as much from the nonpsychiatric subjects.

STYLES OF EMOTIONAL EXPRESSION

Let us now return to the comment of the science editor that began our study of the expression of feeling. Was she correct in assuming that her colleague's aloof, detached way of speaking was due to his infrequent use of *expressions of feeling?* Probably not. We now know that there are many verbal categories involved in conveying emotion. *Expressions of feeling* is only one of them and, perhaps, not even the most important. In discussing the data derived from normal individuals of different ages and both sexes, as well as from groups of psychologically impaired speakers, we have sensed that there are probably *styles* of emotional expression. Some individuals may convey feeling by using evaluative and adverbial enhancing expressions, others by directly engaging the listener.

I do not wish to leave the subject of emotional expression without reemphasizing my conviction that *adverbial intensifiers*, a new category in our verbal system, seems to be most useful in reflecting certain personality traits. Used frequently by most speakers and relatively easy to score, this category is destined to play an important role in future studies. As a marker for distinguishing males from females, *adverbial intensifiers* seems to be more powerful than the categories used for this purpose in my previous publications.

Figure 4.2 demonstrates that in all psychologically impaired groups containing men and women, the mean values for females

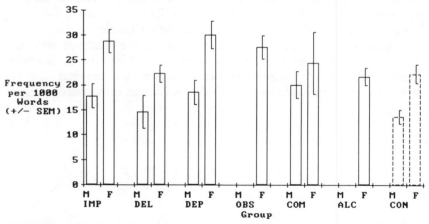

FIGURE 4.2 Use of adverbial intensifiers as a function of sex and diagnostic category. *(IMP = Impulsives; DEL = Delusionals; DEP = Depressives; OBS = Obese Binge-Eaters; COM = Compulsives; ALC = Alcoholics; CON = Controls)*

exceeded those of the males in the *adverbial intensifiers* category. The usefulness of *adverbial intensifiers* as a marker for gender is not extinguished by pathology.

SUMMARY

In this chapter, we have taken a step toward demonstrating that emotion can be conveyed by choice of grammatical structures. Naive judges were able to agree among themselves that when thematic content is controlled for, certain ways of combining words can increase the emotional impact of a message. We were then able to show that this manner of communicating emotion changes at different stages of life among normal people. Some of the reasons why children and adolescents appear to be more open with their feelings were clarified. Women's reputation for being more expressive, "here and now" speakers seems to be well earned.

There still remain many problems to investigate in the area of emotional expression. How can genuine emotion be distinguished from contrived feeling? How can a deeply felt feeling be distinguished from a more superficial one? Clinicians frequently make these distinctions, but they do not lend themselves to easy experimental investigation.

There is, finally, the whole problem of distinguishing different qualities of emotion—love, anger, joy, and so on. This is an extremely complex matter for reasons I have already discussed. We have been content to deal with emotion as a single variable.

In Chapter 5, we shall touch on emotion from a different perspective when we consider the language of intimacy. There we shall study some of the powerful regressive forces affecting grammatical choices when we trace some of the vicissitudes of human relationships.

CHAPTER 5

Intimacy and Familiarity

DAVID AND SAM—AN INTIMATE RELATIONSHIP

Several years ago, a middle-aged man I was treating in intensive psychotherapy—I shall call him David—was planning a weekend trip to another city in order to visit his older brother, Sam. A successful engineer, David had enjoyed an extremely close relationship with Sam from early childhood through young adulthood. Choice of careers, marriage, and certain family conflicts had caused the once close brothers to become alienated from each other. During the previous 10 years, David and Sam rarely saw each other more than once a year, usually at a family celebration or party.

In the course of therapy, David realized how much he missed the closeness he once shared with Sam and decided to have a heart-to-heart talk with his brother. With the insights acquired in psychotherapy, David hoped to reduce the distance between them. The planned trip would enable David to spend an entire day with Sam and explore the reasons for their alienation from each other. David was excited by the idea of a confrontation with Sam and left Baltimore in high spirits.

When I saw him after his return from the brief trip, David expressed extreme disappointment with the results of his encounter with his brother. Although Sam had been friendly and hospitable, David insisted that something crucial was missing. The psychotherapy session continued somewhat as follows:

DAVID:　Sam doesn't remember.

W.W.:　What doesn't Sam remember?

DAVID:　The language. Sam doesn't remember the language. That's what kept us close all those years.

W.W.:　What language?

DAVID:　What language? Our language. It's strange but I've been coming to see you for two years and the language has never come up here. Sam and I had a special language—a secret language. Nobody else understood it, not even our parents. We developed it when we were real small and used it until we drifted apart in our 20s. I tried to talk to Sam in our old language and he said he didn't remember any secret language, didn't know what I was talking about. I can't believe it! How could he have forgotten the language?

W.W.:　Tell me about the secret language.

With considerable difficulty and embarrassment, David described several aspects of the secret language that had once united him with Sam. Similar in structure to most family codes, the secret language had gestural, vocal, and verbal characteristics. A slight, hardly visible flaring of the nostrils indicated displeasure as did the baring of the upper teeth. Pleasurable anticipation was communicated by a clicking noise resulting from the rapid separation and closing of the lips. There were many such signals.

A rather complicated series of verbal cues were part of the brothers' secret language. There were secret names for parents and certain relatives and neighbors. Sexual activities, such as intercourse and masturbation, had special names as did the male and female genitalia. Although letter reversals accounted for some of the secret words, most of the verbal code arose from shared experiences. One of the many words for sexual intercourse, for example, was "Abner," a verbal creation that owed its origin to a sexually active farmhand whom the brothers had met during a summer vacation.

Perhaps the most interesting and inaccessible part of the brothers' language was the use of musical messages. The lyrics of many of the popular songs of their youthful days were changed into personal messages. It was then sufficient merely to sing or hum the melody in order to convey a secret thought in the presence of other family members or neighbors.

It would be tempting to speculate about the reasons why secret languages develop to a greater extent in certain families than in others, but I do not want to be diverted from our task of describing the language of intimacy. Whatever else characterized David's childhood relationship with Sam, it was clearly a close, intimate one. So long as the relationship continued to be close, their secret language endured, even into adulthood. David correctly interpreted Sam's refusal to acknowledge the existence of their special language as an unwillingness to resume their former close relationship.

THE DEVELOPMENT OF AN INTIMATE LANGUAGE

As a student of verbal behavior, I pondered David's experience. What *is* the relationship between language and intimacy? *Is* it possible to describe the closeness of a relationship by certain speech variables?

Let us begin our analysis of the language of intimacy by carefully defining the elements of David and Sam's special family code. As usual, we shall focus almost entirely upon the verbal aspects of their communication.

1. Most of the messages transmitted in their special language could not be understood by others, even by other members of their family. The language of intimacy is, therefore, exclusive. Closeness is achieved, in part, by keeping others out.

2. The development of an intimate language requires shared experiences. Most of the verbal, vocal, and gestural aspects of intimate language can be traced to events jointly experienced by those who speak it.

3. The development of an intimate language is always associated with the use of *elliptical expressions*. I wish to remind readers whose memory of grammar is a bit rusty that *ellipsis* means the omission from a sentence of a word or words that would complete the meaning of the statement. A sentence like, "The marathon will be held on the 15th" is an elliptical remark. The reader or listener is assumed to know *which* marathon the writer or speaker has in mind, *what* month and year he is referring to, and so on.

The more shared knowledge and experience two individuals have, the more likely they are to use elliptical expressions when communicating and the less likely they are to be understood by outsiders. Collier and Horowitz (1984), in their biography of the Kennedy family, described the private language of John and Robert Kennedy as follows: "There was . . . almost a special language between them. It went beyond the staccato sentences and broad vowels of their Massachusetts upbringing; it was a private talk of ellipsis and intuition." Lem Billings, a close friend of John Kennedy, is quoted as saying, "It was strange to hear them have a conversation. Neither of them ever got out a complete sentence. They were on the same wavelength to such a degree, they interrupted to finish each other's thoughts" (p. 288).

4. As a relationship grows in intimacy, an inexorable process of *condensation* takes place so that the same message can be transmitted with fewer and fewer gestural, vocal, and verbal clues. In the case of David and Sam, for example, expressing displeasure by a barely perceptible flaring of the nostrils was the end of an evolutionary process that began with a much more obvious message— the baring of both upper and lower teeth and the forceful flaring of the nostrils. The brothers' use of "Abner" to mean sexual intercourse was also the end state of a process of condensation. The original expression was "Good old Abner Thomas." Although condensation may serve to make the private language of intimates even more esoteric to outsiders, the process is not motivated entirely by a desire for exclusiveness.

5. As a relationship grows in intimacy, there is a simplification of communication so that complicated grammatical devices disappear, and verbal messages are replaced by vocalizations and gestures. Lovers and spouses can often indicate a desire for sexual intercourse by simply making a certain sound or gesture. At the beginning of a romantic relationship, such familiarity would either be misunderstood or resented.

6. Pet names are always part of an intimate relationship. Special names may be used even in the presence of other, nonintimate persons.

7. Attempts by nonintimates to learn the language of a closely related couple or group will lead to the coining of new private expressions. This phenomenon is sometimes observed in cases where parents try to "bridge the generation gap" and become closer to their teenaged children. In these situations, the well-meaning parents do not understand that excluding other members of the family— particularly the parents—is one of the reasons for the development of the private language in the first place (Shapiro, 1979).

8. Most of the special language of intimacy develops during the early phase of the relationship. When the relationship reaches a plateau, relatively few new private messages are encoded. As an intimate relationship cools, the use of private expressions becomes less frequent. Sometimes, as in the case of David and Sam, the use of an intimate language may be completely abandoned (Hopper, Knapp, and Scott, 1981).

9. There is an enormous emotional investment in private, intimate expressions. The "good feeling" that adult family members have when reassembling at reunions and parties is, to some extent, related to the use of the family language. Social alienation is frequently associated with the inability or lack of opportunity to communicate with anybody in a private language.

"Getting To Know You"

As the relationship between verbal behavior and intimacy began to preoccupy me, I found myself listening carefully to other people's conversations. What has particularly fascinated me are the conversations between newly introduced people. Certain newly acquainted individuals seem to "hit it off" immediately and begin the process of forming a close relationship, whether it be a friendship or a romance. Other pairs appear to be uncomfortable when introduced. They look for the first opportunity to disengage and go their separate ways.

What *are* the verbal and nonverbal reflections of "hitting it off?" After observing the behavior of newly introduced couples in both natural and laboratory settings, I have pieced together the following picture of a rapidly developing relationship.

Couples who "hit it off" stand or sit closely together, often positioning themselves in such a way so as to prevent others from intruding into their conversations. There is usually a great deal of smiling, head nodding, and direct gazing. If forced to stand—at cocktail parties, for example—a pair that is "hitting it off" may drift to the periphery of the room in order to decrease the possibility of interruption by others. Attempts by outsiders to join in the conversation are generally discouraged in both nonverbal and verbal ways. The increasingly intimate pair may refuse to change their body positions to physically include newcomers in a circle. They may neglect to introduce other guests to each other or continue their conversation as if nobody else were present.

When seated, the "hitting it off" pair are more likely to sit side-by-side rather than in the more confrontational face-to-face position. Pairs who are not "hitting it off," who are clearly uncomfortable with each other, tend to stand further from each other, gaze less, do not seek the side-by-side sitting position, and, far from trying to exclude others, seem almost frantically to be looking around for somebody to rescue them from an uncomfortable encounter.

What about the verbal reflections of "hitting it off?" Couples who are drawn to each other, after being introduced, quickly find mutually interesting subjects to discuss. In certain cases, these common interests appear to derive quite naturally from similarities in their backgrounds. In other cases, common interests are found despite radically different backgrounds. A mysterious attraction appears to drive couples of different backgrounds to find common interests even though none seem to exist.

The most interesting verbal sign of "hitting it off" is the use of elliptical devices. With astonishing speed, members of a "successful" pair will use shared knowledge, generally obtained during the first few seconds of the interaction, to construct sentences that are unintelligible to outsiders. "Unsuccessful" pairs are far less apt to use ellipsis. Their conversations can easily be understood by others no matter how long they have known each other.

Examples of Intimate and Nonintimate Conversations. Let us compare a real life conversation in which a newly introduced pair is "hitting it off" with one in which the participants are known to each other but are not intimate. The first conversation I overheard at a cocktail party during a medical meeting. Dr. Jones approached Dr. Smith and started to speak:

JONES: You must be Ed Smith. I recognized you from Jerry Klein's description. I'm Tim Jones. Jerry and I were classmates in medical school.
SMITH: Of course. Tell me, how is Jerry? Has he forgotten Margaret yet?
JONES: I'm afraid not. She gave him quite a turn.

The reader will note that a listener overhearing the conversation after Jones' opening remarks would be unable to understand the comments of either participant. Jones and Smith, after knowing each other for less than 15 seconds, have effectively excluded the other party guests from their conversation. The two doctors' common knowledge has been derived from a shared acquaintanceship with a third person.

The following conversation, overheard while waiting on line to buy theater tickets, shows that shared knowledge prior to the first meeting is not necessary to the quick use of elliptical sentences in initial encounters.

GENTLEMAN I: Excuse me, I didn't mean to step on your toes.
GENTLEMAN II: No problem. It's awfully crowded here.
GENTLEMAN I: If I had known, I wouldn't have come.
GENTLEMAN II: You would have saved money and time.
GENTLEMAN I: And you, some toes!

The above example demonstrates how quickly two compatible strangers can resort to the use of elliptical expressions without having to allude to experiences shared prior to their first meeting. An observer overhearing the conversation could not understand the two gentlemen if he missed the first exchange of comments.

At this point, the reader may protest that all conversationalists sooner or later resort to ellipsis even if they are not congenial. Not so. Several months ago, I overheard the following fragment of a conversation in an outdoor Baltimore restaurant. A couple seated at the table next to mine were eating their desserts, so I could assume that their conversation was at least half an hour old.

MAN: I hope you don't mind my saying this, Susan, but I can't stand your sister. I hope I never see her again.
WOMAN: Oh, my sister's not that bad.
MAN: Your sister is so different from you. I think your father was so wise to leave the management of his estate in your hands when he died.
WOMAN: (laughs)
(An airplane is heard flying overhead)
MAN: Do you see that plane, Susan? When I was in the Air Force, I learned a great deal about that particular fighter plane. Do you realize that your father's research made it possible to build that plane?

The reader will note that the conversation involves two people who have previously met. Yet their remarks contain nothing that cannot be easily understood by a stranger. The conversation continued to the end of the dinner without any elliptical comments being made by either of the participants. I have come to believe that individuals holding such conversations are not on intimate terms. Years ago, I had dinner in the home of a professional colleague. His wife and two children were present. When I left, I had a strange feeling that all was not right between my colleague and his wife although they were polite and gracious with each other. Something was missing. None of the elements of intimate conversation were present when they addressed each other. There were few elliptical expressions, no knowing smiles, no mysterious gestures. They were divorced shortly afterward.

Verbal Condensation in Intimate Relationships

I have already referred to the importance of condensation in intimate conversations. Students of verbal behavior have noted that the development of a close relationship is characterized by the replacement of fully deployed syntactic structures by elliptical expressions, vocalizations, and gestures. Complicated messages can be transmitted among intimates with few or no words (Bradac, 1983). I gave several examples of this phenomenon when discussing the relationship between David and Sam. Here is another.

Dr. Moran, a colleague on the faculty of the University of Maryland School of Medicine, performs an interesting ritual on many mornings when he arrives at work during the spring and summer months. He approaches Jack, the maintenance man, and either utters the sound "Aaah," with an accompanying look of disgust or a triumphant "Aha" with his thumbs pointed upward. Jack responds with a sad shake of his head to the first greeting and with a broad smile to the second. Curious about the meaning of these enigmatic encounters, I asked Dr. Moran for an explanation. He told me that both he and Jack are fanatical followers of the Baltimore Orioles baseball team. Dr. Moran's disgusted exclamation can be translated as follows: "The Orioles lost again last night and it was a game they should have won." The triumphant greeting means, "The Orioles won a game they could have lost. Why can't they do that more often?" More ordinary wins and losses do not elicit these particular greetings from Dr. Moran.

Knowing about my interest in verbal behavior, Dr. Moran was good enough to explain that at the beginning of his relationship with Jack, he actually would make long verbal statements about the Orioles' games. As their relationship evolved, the remarks became shorter and shorter until the entire message could be transmitted without words.

The Clinical Significance of Ellipsis

Since the use of elliptical expressions depends upon knowledge shared by two or more people, the false assumption of shared knowledge can lead to the inappropriate use of ellipsis. Psychiatric patients who have lost touch with reality frequently use elliptical expressions in situations where no shared knowledge exists. The following example of a patient's inappropriate use of ellipsis was noted during a course on interviewing techniques that I give to a small group of first-year medical students. Each session of the course is devoted to a patient interview conducted by a medical student. The patients used for the interviews have had no previous contact with the students.

MEDICAL STUDENT: How do you do, Mr. Conway. I'm Jeff Simpson, a first-year medical student. What circumstances brought you to the hospital?

PATIENT: (Smiles) Perhaps I should ask you that question. Martha and Mr. Lindstrom have managed things very well.

MEDICAL STUDENT: Martha? Mr. Lindstrom? Who are they?

PATIENT: (Smiles) I think I've already said enough. There is no reason to continue this farce.

As the reader has undoubtedly surmised, the medical student was interviewing a delusional patient who assumed that the student was part of a plot that led to his hospitalization. He believed that the medical student knew the identities of his wife, Martha, and his landlord, Mr. Lindstrom. Thinking that he and the student had shared knowledge about the events leading to his hospitalization, he quite naturally used elliptical expressions.

The inappropriate use of ellipsis is common among psychotic patients and is of great diagnostic importance. Elliptical expressions can be used inappropriately by nonpsychotic persons however. Individuals who have lived most of their lives in tightly-knit, lower-class neighborhoods frequently assume that their relatives and friends are known to everyone, even people living outside their communities. This phenomenon has been described by the British sociologist, Basil Bernstein (1959; 1960). According to Bernstein, social relations lead to two styles of verbal communication, involving both syntactic and lexical levels. These codes are called *restricted* and *elaborated*. Restricted codes are characteristic of the lower socioeconomic classes, tend to be concrete, rigid, and contain few grammatical options. Inappropriate elliptical expressions are apt to appear in the speech of individuals with restricted linguistic codes, as in the following example. The patient, a young woman admitted to a psychiatric inpatient unit for the treatment of a personality disorder, was from one of Baltimore's closely-knit ethnic neighborhoods.

MEDICAL STUDENT: How do you do, Miss Young. I'm Ellen Atkins, a first-year medical student. What brings you to the hospital?

PATIENT: Well, it's real complicated. Mom and I were arguing in the kitchen and Jimmy walks in, starts mouthing off, and—

MEDICAL STUDENT: Excuse me. Who is Jimmy?

PATIENT: Oh, he's my boyfriend. Well, I'm getting really upset. I said, "You stay out of this, Jimmy. I got some things I want to say to Mom. You look after Tammy."

MEDICAL STUDENT: Tammy?

PATIENT: She's my baby.

The reader will note that the patient, although not psychotic, assumed that the medical student had more knowledge of her situation and of the people in her life than she did. She assumed that her little world was everybody's world. Since Americans tend to be ethnocentric, even middle-class U.S. tourists sometimes inappropriately use elliptical expressions when traveling in foreign countries. They are surprised to learn that citizens of other countries have never heard of important places and people from back home.

Ellipsis as a Developmental Milestone

Readers who have children or who work with children know that preschoolers frequently use ellipsis when talking to adults. They do not always fully explain what they mean. We assume that this is because small children think adults are omniscient and do not require explanations. In my studies of children's free speech, I have learned that school-aged children—those in kindergarten and above—do not, in fact, inappropriately use ellipsis in their monologues. The following examples from two 6-year-old girls are typical in this respect. The reader will note how carefully the two

young pupils introduce material that may be unfamiliar to the research technician:

FEMALE PUPIL I: My name's Michelle and my mother is a teacher and my
father is an engineer. And I got a cousin and, well,
there's a lot of cousins and a lot of my friends at
———— School. I like to go to school and one day
when I grow up, I'll be able to be a movie star.

FEMALE PUPIL II: I don't have much to say. My daddy gave me a watch to
put on my wrist and my friend and my mom taught me
how to see minutes. . . . I went to Seattle to my
grandmother's and grandfather's before I came to Baltimore. It was summertime and they were fixing up the
house and painting. When it was fall, I went to school.

The reader will agree, I believe, that the above free speech remarks can be easily understood by listeners completely unfamiliar
with the children who made them. This is not surprising. Children
who have been deemed ready to pursue a systematic education
must be able to separate themselves and their past experiences from
those of their teachers and fellow pupils.

The Importance of Exclusion in
Intimate Relationships

Although most of what I have reported about intimate communication has been described in the literature, the phenomenon of exclusion, as a necessary part of intimate behavior, has not been
stressed by investigators. To be sure, literary artists have sometimes
emphasized the importance of exclusion in the development of intimate relationships. In his play, *The Misanthrope*, Moliere has Alceste reject an offer of friendship from someone he considered to
be too friendly with others (1954). (See p. 72.) Moliere seemed to be
suggesting that what could so easily be shared was not worth very
much. My own observations suggest that intimate conversations are
necessarily secretive and are invariably associated with body movements, hand gestures, vocalizations, whispering, and elliptical expressions that are designed to exclude others. Why is this so?
Intimate relationships necessarily involve a certain regression of
thinking and behavior that cannot openly be expressed to nonintimates, perhaps out of fear of ridicule. Intimate forms of address
may also be a way of possessing a friend or lover. The French put it

well when they say, "Les amoureux sont seuls au monde" (lovers live in a world of their own). True intimacy means more than two individuals achieving closeness. It also means the exclusion of everyone else.

Codes and Dialects

Until now, we have been dealing for the most part with intimate conversations involving two people. But there are a number of situations in which groups of individuals having something in common develop special languages that exclude other people. In certain cases, a special language may be spoken by people practicing a certain profession. If the vocabulary of a professional or occupational jargon reflects changing and widespread ways of thinking and behaving, its expressions may become useful metaphors in the ordinary language of a people. Expressions such as "getting to first base" and "striking out" are used metaphorically by Americans who have little or no interest in baseball. More recently, many colorful terms borrowed from the field of communications, such as "input," "connecting with people," and "networking" have become part of ordinary English.

Certain groups develop secret languages with the conscious purpose of excluding others. Slang expressions may develop out of a group's need to establish a certain solidarity (Enkvist, 1973). If the particular ideas and practices of a group become acceptable to the larger society, some of its slang expressions may attain widespread use.

I have already alluded to the special language of children and adolescents. In the process of attaining independence from their parents, young people will often develop exclusive languages so that they may communicate among themselves without their parents being able to understand them. In their development of secret codes, Shapiro (1979) has compared the behavior of children to that of "a new ethnic group" (p. 145). Wise parents respect their children's need for privacy and do not attempt to use the jargon of the young.

The spontaneous development of private expressions can be extremely rapid. How rapid? Many years ago, I met a young Swiss gentleman on an ocean liner sailing to Europe. He had just spent 6 months in the United States and was returning to Switzerland. Milo invited me to visit him in his home in Lucerne. When I arrived about a month later, he introduced me to his group of friends and we went hiking in the mountains. Milo confessed to me that he could not understand certain of his friends' slang expressions that had apparently developed during his 6-month absence.

Clubs and fraternal organizations always have verbal secrets of some kind that only members share. These may be passwords or greetings of some kind. Mythology is full of stories of the magic power of secret words and names.

Intimacy in the Theater

One of the most difficult technical tasks of a playwright is to present to an audience an intimate relationship between two or more characters. Our discussion of the language of intimacy has taught us that intimates speak a language that is, at least in part, unintelligible to others. How can an already developed close relationship be presented to an audience in a way that is both believable and intelligible?

One answer to our question is that playwrights often fail in attempts to depict intimate relationships as they are in real life. A certain stilted and awkward dialogue may result. There are several devices that "realistic" playwrights use when dealing with intimate relationships. One is to have the characters discuss certain past experiences when appearing for the first time on the stage. Arthur Miller uses this technique when Biff and his brother first appear together in *Death of a Salesman*. Such a device is believable only if the two intimates have been separated for a period of time, as is the case with the two brothers in Miller's play (1949).

Another technique, used by Neil Simon in *Brighton Beach Memoirs* (1984), is to allow an otherwise natural dialogue to be explained to the audience by one of the characters in the play, who temporarily leaves the scene of action and communicates directly with the audience. In this way, events and remarks not clear to the audience can be explained by the "reporter." A third device, sometimes used by Eugene O'Neill, is to have the actors speak their thoughts aloud directly to the audience. In this way, several players can act as reporters and help explain otherwise incomprehensible comments among intimates.

The Language of Lovemaking— A Project for the Future

Whether the reader considers lovemaking to be the most intimate of behaviors or an activity carried out in a specific and highly aroused affective state, its nonverbal and verbal reflections are extremely interesting. Although most adults have engaged in sexual intercourse, there have been, to my knowledge, no systematic attempts to analyze the language of lovemaking. The loss of boundaries during orgasm is a unique psychological and physiological phenomenon and deserves careful study.

I have attempted, without success, to obtain from intimate behavior programs verbatim verbal data from couples engaged in sexual intercourse. The various programs, including the one directed by Masters and Johnson, simply have not collected free speech samples from their clients.

Not having access to systematically gathered verbal data, we must make do with anecdotal reports. Novelists have certainly given us many explicit accounts of lovemaking and we can assume that these descriptions are based upon real-life observations.

James Joyce, who possessed one of the best ears for dialogue among twentieth century novelists, has provided us with interesting dialogue from sexually aroused individuals. In his analysis of the speech patterns of the characters in Joyce's *Ulysses*, Steinberg (1973) concluded that sexual arousal is associated with a decrease of *negatives* and a significant simplification of grammatical structures. In many ways, Steinberg's results were similar to those I reported for individuals speaking while in a state of extreme anger (Weintraub, 1981).

Relying upon anecdotal data, I would suggest that the verbal reflections of lovemaking include the following: (1) a decrease in the frequency of such "sophisticated" grammatical devices as *qualifiers, retractors,* and *explainers;* (2) a decrease in *nonpersonal references* and an increase in the use of other "feelings" categories, such as *expressions of feeling, evaluators, adverbial intensifiers, direct references, commands,* and the *present tense;* and (3) a decrease in the use of *negatives* as well as an increase in the use of "positive" expressions, such as "Yes," "Okay," "Of course," and so on.

PSEUDOINTIMACY OR FAMILIARITY

More than any other people in the world, Americans do not carefully distinguish true intimacy from familiarity. Perhaps because we are a very mobile society and therefore need ways of feeling quickly at home in new settings, we often fail to use forms of address designed to protect the dignity of strangers. When I first arrived in Baltimore many years ago, I was astonished to hear saleswomen in large department stores address me as "Honey." I am sure that such familiarity was innocent and meant to convey a friendly spirit, but, having grown up in New York City, I regarded "intimate" approaches on the part of total strangers to be intrusive and inappropriate. There are situations when familiarity on the part of salespeople is not so innocent but is part of a strategy of interpersonal domination, a subject we shall consider in more detail later in the chapter.

How do we distinguish familiarity from true intimacy? In pseudointimacy, or familiarity, one or both members of a pair may use forms of address or make certain demands upon the other without having developed a close, affectionate relationship based upon shared experiences. Depending upon the psychological needs of a person, familiarity may be welcomed or resented. If resented, the verbal exchange will quickly become more formal.

How do the verbal reflections of familiarity differ from those of true intimacy? Primarily by the relative paucity of ellipsis. Without shared knowledge and experience, the familiar member of a pair must use fully deployed grammatical constructions in order to make himself understood.

As I have suggested above, salespeople frequently use familiarity as an attempt to create an atmosphere more favorable to commercial success. Many potential customers have a very difficult time resisting sales pitches when approached in a "friendly," familiar way. Yet, in order not to allow familiarity to influence his judgment, it is important for the customer to keep the salesperson at an appropriate distance, at least until a decision about the business at hand has been made. The best way of doing this is to discourage the use of first names as well as talk about personal matters. Resisting pseudointimacy in commercial relationships can help us avoid being trapped by salespeople who exploit our need to be liked.

I know of no better distinction between familiarity and intimacy than that described by Moliere in *The Misanthrope* (1954). He has Alceste reject a request for "immediate friendship" with these words:

> Sir, it's a very great honor you extend:
> But friendship is a sacred thing, my friend;
> It would be profanation to bestow
> The name of friend on one you hardly know.
> All parts are better played when well-rehearsed;
> Let's put off friendship, and get acquainted first.

We may discover it would be unwise
To try to make our natures harmonize.[*]

OTHER FORMS OF VERBAL DOMINATION

Using familiar forms of address with strangers is not the only way of dominating a conversation. Domineering individuals often speak in loud, harsh voices, submissive persons in softer, sometimes barely audible tones. A common way of dominating a conversation may be simply to talk more, to refuse to allow others to share equally in the dialogue (Courtright, Millar, and Rogers-Millar, 1979). Rude, domineering speakers may frequently interrupt others, and in extreme cases, give commands or curse. As we shall see in Chapter 10, Lyndon Johnson, one of the more domineering of our post-World War II Presidents, used many of these devices when speaking to reporters. Johnson employed yet another effective intimidating method. When annoyed by a question he didn't want to answer, he would give an extremely curt response, one that bordered on the impolite.

In marital communication, the dominating partner may answer for the spouse when conversing with a third person. In most cases, it is the husband who answers when his wife is asked a question (Key, 1975).

One of the more interesting and subtle ways of dominating a conversation is to use many conjunctions. The use of conjunctions or connectives enables a speaker to avoid ending a sentence, thus denying the listener an opportunity to talk. By not lowering his voice, he fails to give a "turn-taking" signal. He simply drones on and on. Obsessional people are often guilty of this annoying habit. In their free-speech monologues, they tend to exceed nonobsessional individuals in the sheer length of their utterances. Of the post-World War II Presidents, Kennedy, Johnson, and Carter were most apt to dominate interchanges with reporters by their use of connectives.

Victims of verbal aggression are often at a loss as to how to react. I advise them to quickly put an end to all varieties of verbal assault, whether overt or subtle. If the domineering behavior is polite, as in the case of the overuse of connectives, the victim should try to interrupt and make his or her point of view known to the domineering speaker. If this approach is unsuccessful, the victim should

---

[*] *Source:* From *The Misanthrope* by Moliere, p. 22, 1954.

simply excuse him or herself and end the conversation. Domineering speakers who are rude, that is, those who interrupt, curse, or command, should not be tolerated. Their rudeness should be pointed out and the conversation ended.

Passive Resistance to Verbal Aggression

An interesting form of resistance to verbal aggression is sometimes used by individuals who are in a weak position vis-a-vis the domineering speaker. An employee dealing with a domineering boss, for example, may not be able to walk away and keep his job. Such victims, if astute, may resort to the kind of passive resistance I described in the introductory chapter. The weaker speaker simply appears to go along with what is being demanded, but carefully qualifies his or her approval of the stronger speaker's demands.

NONVERBAL TECHNIQUES OF DOMINATION

Although we are dealing primarily with verbal forms of dominance, some mention of nonverbal forms of dominating conversations may be interesting to the reader. They include taking the head position of a rectangular table, occupying a higher seat or podium when speaking, and keeping the other person waiting. Some domineering individuals have their secretaries telephone victims and keep them waiting while the Big Shot is finishing some other business. The only way for a victim to deal with such boorish behavior is to hang up before the Big Shot picks up the phone—providing, of course, that he or she is not your boss!

PSEUDOINTIMACY IN CLINICAL WORK

Regretfully, familiarity has found its way into clinical psychiatric work. The U.S. penchant for informality has been reinforced during the past two decades by the strong humanistic movement in clinical psychiatry. Many psychotherapists have been under pressure to present themselves as "real human beings" rather than as professionals providing a clinical service for a fee. Various forms of pseudointimacy have resulted, including informal dress, familiar forms of address, and socializing with patients. In extreme cases, the wish for an informal relationship has gotten out of hand and therapists have become involved in sexual relationships with patients.

I have noticed the growing informality between professionals and patients during my interviewing seminars with medical students and psychiatric residents. What should be the most routine part of an initial interview—the exchange of names during the introduction—frequently turns out to be an occasion for offending a patient. Calling patients by their first names without their permission is symptomatic of the increasing familiarity of U.S. psychiatry. Nothing makes me wince more than hearing a young psychiatrist-in-training address a middle-aged patient by his first name. "Hello, Tom, I'm Bill." Or even worse, "Hello, Tom, I'm Dr. Prescott." I teach my students to always address adults and older adolescents as Mr. and Ms. unless they have been given permission to do otherwise. To assume the right to call a patient by his or her first name is to show an attitude that is both insensitive and patronizing.

SUMMARY

In this chapter, we have presented a smorgasbord of anecdotes illustrating some of the facets of intimate language. Our remarks should be seen more as hypotheses requiring confirmation than as definitive statements about the subject of intimacy. The literature on intimacy contains almost no experimental work on natural conversations among intimates. Most of the laboratory work has consisted of experimental subjects giving their opinions about how they behave in intimate conversations. The procedural problems involved in the analysis of natural conversations are formidable. I am presently conducting research with married couples, attempting to define differences between their choices of grammatical structures and those of less intimate couples. The preliminary data are congruent with the observations reported in this chapter.

In Chapter 7, we shall be looking very closely at the Presidential news conferences of the post-World War II U.S. Chief Executives. Among many other problems the President faces at these gatherings is that of how to present to a live television audience relationships with journalists that may be close without distracting the viewers. After all, the President is not meeting the reporters for the first time. Several of them may be very good friends, may even have worked in the Presidential electoral campaign. Yet to do the "natural thing" and by gesture or word show signs of intimacy would detract from the seriousness and clarity of the news conference. As we shall see, different Presidents have handled this problem in different ways, ranging from inappropriate familiarity to extreme reserve. Before embarking on our studies of Presidential speech styles, let us turn our attention to a method of assessing personality traits of individual speakers by means of verbal analysis. This will be the subject of Chapter 6.

Verbal Reflections of Personality

INTRODUCTION

We are now prepared to apply some of the lessons we have learned in the previous chapters to the analysis of the personality characteristics of individual speakers. In this chapter, I shall describe the method I use to associate preferences for certain grammatical structures with clinically important patterns of behavior.

Prior to 1975, my attempts to correlate speech and personality were limited to groups of psychologically impaired patients sharing patterns of symptomatic behavior. During that year, a psycholinguistics research team at the University of Michigan challenged me to create personality profiles for two speakers, based entirely upon their 10-minute free speech monologues. The speech samples were prepared by the University of Michigan researchers in the manner described in Chapter 1, and I was sent only verbatim typed transcripts of the electronically recorded monologues. No other information about the speakers was given to me.

After scoring the transcripts in the usual way, I attempted written personality evaluations of the two speakers and sent them to my University of Michigan colleagues. After comparing my reports with independent assessments of the speakers' personalities, the Michigan group concluded that my method had the ability "to accurately tap certain important personality dimensions" (J. Binder, personal communication, 1975).

ANALYZING THE WATERGATE TRANSCRIPTS

Encouraged by the results of this pilot study, I decided to take advantage of the publication of the Watergate transcripts to continue my analysis of individual speakers. The Watergate transcripts presented students of verbal behavior with a unique opportunity. To my knowledge, never before in history had spontaneous conversations involving important political leaders been electronically recorded and made available to the public.

I reasoned that since the participants in the Watergate affair could be assumed to have been under considerable stress during most of the published conversations, the transcripts should contain pertinent data relative to the adaptive patterns, as reflected in their styles of speaking, of the four individuals whose remarks made up the bulk of the recorded material. Using my verbal categories, I compared samples of speech attributed to Richard Nixon, A. R. Haldeman, John Ehrlichman, and John Dean with those of a normal control group and with populations of delusional, impulsive, depressive, and compulsive psychiatric patients. My results indicated no abnormal verbal behavior for either Dean or Ehrlichman. President Nixon could not be distinguished from the depressed patients in any of the verbal categories and deviated from the impulsives in only one. Haldeman's style appeared to be abnormal, but unlike any of the patient groups I have studied (Weintraub, 1981).

CARTER AND REAGAN COMPARED

I recently published another verbal analysis of political leaders. Using samples of their Presidential news conference remarks, I compared the spontaneous speaking styles of Jimmy Carter and Ronald Reagan. In my verbal analysis, I included certain speculations about the personality traits of the two Presidents, including, in Ronald Reagan's case, an attempt to delineate areas of vulnerability to stress (Weintraub, 1986).

RECOGNITION VERSUS UNDERSTANDING IN CHARACTER ANALYSIS

The reader is undoubtedly familiar with so-called psychobiographical approaches to historical figures. The methodology of psychobiography, which is usually psychoanalytically inspired, consists of substituting data gathered by historical research for free associations from the couch. Although the data in the biographer's possession have not been obtained by psychoanalytic methods, that is, by free association, attempts are nevertheless made to construct elaborate psychodynamic and psychogenetic formulations. In my judgment such analyses necessarily lack validity. In a genuine psychoanalysis, a patient's distortion of the past is irrelevant since the analyst is concerned with psychic reality. Interpretations can be validated by the patient's associative responses. In a psychobiography, the accuracy of historical data is vital if the biographer is not to cross the line between historical reality and fiction. The absence of the biographer's subject makes validation of psychological interpretations of intent impossible. Even in the most skillful hands, psychoanalytic biography has a flavor of wild analysis. In the search for meaning, the psychoanalytic biographer deals with derivatives of a finite number of universal drives and phase-specific conflicts. The result is to demonstrate what the great and famous have in common with lesser individuals rather than how they differ from them. As understanding of the historical figure advances, the ability to distinguish him or her from others diminishes.

The method we shall use stresses recognition rather than meaning. We shall look for those grammatical surface manifestations of personality that can be observed and objectively recorded. The path of recognition leads to differentiation, and, hopefully, to those factors that contribute to achievement.

THE GRAMMATICAL ANALYSIS
OF PERSONALITY

What advantages do grammatical structures have for the investigation of personality traits? Several. First of all, individual preferences for grammatical structures apparently begin to develop in early childhood, just as personality traits do. Like personality traits, grammatical choices have a slow rate of change (Weintraub & Aronson, 1962). This is much less true of preferences for topics and vocabulary that are strongly influenced by a number of situational variables (Laffal, 1965; Steingart & Freedman, 1972). Another advantage of grammatical analysis is the ease with which protocols can be reliably scored. Finally, my colleagues and I have already demonstrated that speakers' grammatical preferences are

associated with clinically significant patterns of symptomatic behavior (Weintraub & Aronson, 1964, 1965, 1967, 1969, 1974).

Which Traits Shall We Investigate?

Once we have decided to approach the study of personality by
analyzing grammatical preferences, the next question is, "Which
traits are we interested in?" To some extent, I have already answered this question in my previous investigative work. In attempting to demonstrate the clinical usefulness of my method, I have
studied populations of patients sharing such characteristics as impulsivity, compulsivity, eating and drinking habits, and delusional
and depressive behavior.

Clearly, the traits and symptomatic behaviors already studied do
not constitute a broad enough base upon which to construct a com-
prehensive personality evaluation. What then should be added? I
propose the following list of personality traits as both sufficiently
inclusive to describe a recognizable human being and suitable for
investigation by means of verbal analysis. After each personality
trait, I shall indicate which of our grammatical categories seem to be
associated with it and, where appropriate, offer examples of how the
presence of the trait in question can be detected in samples of free
speech.

Some Personality Traits Reflected by
Grammatical Choices

1. *Decisiveness.* This trait has already been discussed in Chapter
3. We noted there that preparation for decision can be measured by
the frequency of occurrence of *qualifiers.* In excessive amounts,
qualifying phrases suggest indecisiveness. Once the necessary preparation for action has been completed, the use of the indicative mood
with the personal pronouns *I* or *we*, as subjects of clauses, reflects
the ability to take action and to accept responsibility for it.

2. *Reconsideration.* The ability to reconsider a decision after it
has been made has also been discussed in Chapter 3. We concluded
that reconsideration is best reflected by the use of *retractors* in
moderate amounts.

3. *Impulsivity.* This trait has been extensively investigated in a
psychiatric patient group (Weintraub & Aronson, 1964). A greater
than average use of *retractors* distinguishes impulsive individuals
from those not having this character trait.

We have also suggested in Chapter 3 that speakers having low *qualifiers and retractors* scores have the capacity to make decisions and to stick to them; high scores in both these categories reflects a paralysis of decision, a tendency to waffle. Clinical examples of problems in decision making have been given in Chapter 3.

Let us now consider several traits associated with the speaker's affective style. The most important for character analysis are *anxious disposition, moodiness, angry disposition,* and *emotional control.*

4. *Anxious Disposition.* An internal rather than an observable condition, anxiety as a reflection of grammatical choice has received scant attention in the literature. Most investigators interested in anxious speech have stressed vocal dynamics rather than verbal behavior (Mahl, 1956; Siegman and Pope, 1965).

Let us approach the subject of anxious disposition by carefully studying the following verbatim excerpt from a 10-minute monologue recorded by a highly anxious female patient:

> I don't know exactly what to say, really, because I—I don't know what subject to talk about. I—I've been very upset at the [ward] meeting this afternoon, so, therefore, I don't say that's a very pleasant subject to speak on. Because I don't like to—to be reminded of things that upset me. So, I don't know what's the—the most recent subject in my mind. So, therefore, it's not pleasant to speak about. So, I don't know what to talk about. Except, that I enjoy my company upstairs with the—with the people I—I'm associated with very much. They're very, very friendly and very [pause] compatible. And I—I enjoy being with them except, of course, I—I don't want to go home anyway so actually it isn't—I suppose it isn't the fact that I enjoy my stay up there particularly, but I just don't want to go home. Because I don't like what's facing me at home when I get there. But I don't know what to say, Doctor, I just feel sort of ridiculous because I don't know what to say, and I don't feel like I want to express my feelings that keep me upset . . . .

The reader will note that this typically anxious patient made frequent use of categories suggesting self-preoccupation ("I" and "me"), defensiveness (*explainers* such as "because" and "therefore"; *negatives* such as "don't"), paralysis of decision (*qualifiers* such as "sort of" and *retractors* such as "except" and "but"), difficulty containing emotion (*personal references* such as "I," *expressions of feeling* such as "I don't like" and "I enjoy," *evaluators* such as "pleasant" and "friendly," *adverbial intensifiers* such as "very" and "really"), and pleas for help (*direct references* such as "I don't know what to say, Doctor").

What characterizes the anxious speaker is the frequent use of *several* of the categories I have noted. It is almost as if the speaker's customary style of containing anxiety has proved inadequate to the stressful situation in which she is performing. She is forced to call upon all the verbal resources available to her.

5. *Moodiness.* We have already identified the principal verbal transmitters of emotion in Chapter 4. They are high scores in the following categories: *I/we* ratio, *adverbial intensifiers, direct references, expressions of feeling, evaluators,* and *personal references.* Mercurial speakers are characterized by a tendency to be *erratic* in their use of emotional categories. Of the post-World War II Presidents we shall study in Part II, Lyndon Johnson and Richard Nixon showed verbal evidence of rapidly shifting moods.

What about evidence of depression in speech? This topic has been extensively researched and the reader is referred to Chapter 4 and a previous publication devoted to the speech of depressed patients (Aronson & Weintraub, 1967b). To summarize our findings, let us recall that speakers with depressive disorders show a verbal pattern that consists of a paucity of speech, a low *nonpersonal references* score and high scores in the following categories: *I, me, direct references, expressions of feeling, negatives, evaluators,* and *adverbial intensifiers.* These scores reflect the depressed speaker's uncontrolled affect (high scores in "emotional" categories), self-preoccupation (high *I* score), dependent needs (high *direct references* and *me* scores), and negativity (high *negatives* score).

The reader may wonder whether this "depressive" verbal pattern holds true for speakers who have a depressive temperament but who are not symptomatic when volunteering samples of speech. While extremes of talkativeness and taciturnity may be moderated in remission, there is no evidence that the other verbal characteristics of depression return to normal (Aronson & Weintraub, 1967b). It is entirely possible that patients with a depressive disposition share certain features of the clinically depressed speech pattern.

6. *Angry Disposition.* Speakers with angry dispositions frequently become irritable during interviews. Occasionally they explode if challenged by the interviewer, as in the following example: Tom, a young violence-prone adult inpatient, lost his ward privileges after fighting with Sam, another patient on the ward. After learning that Sam was not similarly punished, Tom had the following angry outburst when questioned about the incident by his resident-physician during a therapy session:

> How come Sam wasn't restricted when he attacked me and Clayton had to pull him back? Why wasn't he restricted? He's your patient. Why wasn't he

restricted? . . . Bullshit! *You* talk to the patients up there. He was the one who started the god-damned fight. I didn't provoke him . . . . One patient raises a hand to me—one patient—I'll kill him and I'm telling you this now—I'll kill him! . . . Oh, I see, but I get restricted on the ward and he runs loose and you warned me because Sam attacked me, attacked me. . . . I never provoked the man. I just sat there in my chair minding my own business. I didn't scream at him until he got so close to me I had to scream for Clayton to get him away from me. The patient must be suicidal because . . . .

Let us examine the above fragments and see how the angry comments are grammatically formed. The reader will note the complete absence of qualifying phrases. In the heat of extreme anger, all evidence of indecisiveness disappears. Another characteristic of angry discourse is the extreme negativity. Tom's use of *negatives* is about five times that of a normal speaker in a nonangry state. Other verbal findings worthy of note are the use of *rhetorical questions* and *direct references*, indicating an aggressive engagement of the listener. A more complete discussion of the speech pattern associated with anger can be found in *Verbal Behavior* (Weintraub, 1981).

7. *Emotionally Controlled Speakers.* Emotionally controlled individuals tend to have low scores in most or all of the "feelings" categories. Speakers who are perceived as "expressive" or "warm" have high scores in the "emotional" categories. Verbatim examples of emotionally controlled and expressive speakers have been given in Chapter 4.

8. *Oppositional Trait.* The speech of oppositional or stubborn speakers is characterized by the presence of many *negatives*. In the psychiatric groups I have studied, impulsive speakers have used *negatives* more frequently than any other patient population. The following verbatim material has been taken from the monologue of a highly resistant female borderline patient who was admitted to a university psychiatric inpatient service after a series of self-destructive acts:

Nobody's been up to see me. I'm all alone in this world, all by myself. That's why I *don't* care if I'm alone after I get out of here. Because *nobody's* up here, ever comes to see me—*nobody!*—except Charlie is coming this afternoon and Mario, the only two. The only two people that have been up here. *No* relations, *nobody* else, just them. The only people. *No* relations or anything. That would make anybody feel bad. Made me feel bad too. *Can't* do anything about it. People *don't* like you, they just *don't* like you, that's all there is to it. I'm *not* going to worry about it. And I'm *not*—I'm *not* on dope.

During her 10-minute free-speech monologue, this young patient used *five times* the number of *negatives* expressed by normal speakers. *Negatives*, of course, express more than oppositional behavior. In the speech sample just discussed, *negatives* also served the purpose of dramatizing the young woman's message, since they were used to convey a flavor of "all or nothing" or "black and white" thinking.

9. *Controlling Behavior*. This personality characteristic is verbally reflected in at least two ways. Controlling speakers are frequently emotionally controlled; that is, they use "feelings" categories infrequently. During interviews, such speakers may show evidence of extensive preparation (low frequency of *qualifiers*) in order to assure a good public performance.

10. *Histrionic Behavior*. Since this trait suggests the dramatic, those categories that lend themselves to the expression of exaggerating tendencies—*adverbial intensifiers* and *evaluators*—are frequently used by histrionic speakers. The following excerpt from a free-speech monologue recorded by a young female volunteer well illustrates the verbal style of a histrionic person:

> Well, I don't *really* know what to talk about. The first thing I see, I guess, is what I'll talk about—until something else *better* comes into my mind. Gosh! It *really* is—oh—this is *so simple*—wait! All right, I'll talk about clothing, girls' clothing. And—I don't know—I like tweeds, I like bright colors. And I think they *really* make a person look *vibrant* and give them a personality. Because they *add* to a person. Sometimes when a person is *drab* or they don't have a lot—they're quiet or something—the clothes will make a person look *better*. And they *do a lot* for them. . . . This is *just terrible*. I mean—if I had someone else to talk to, I could say something interesting. But when it comes to talking like this, you *just* don't know what to say. Well, here I am sitting—it *really*—it *really* does look *simple*—talking to myself—I *really* feel like an *idiot*.

11. *Achievement*. Speakers for whom achievement is important tend to make frequent use of *I* and *we* (personal pronouns acting on verbs) and infrequent use of *qualifiers* (indicating both careful planning and decisiveness). The following excerpt from a 10-minute monologue of a well-organized female medical student illustrates the verbal style of a high-achieving speaker.

> When I went to do a physical examination (on a male patient), Dr. S informed me that I should have a male attendant present. At first, I felt it was silly because I never had to have this before. However, I was quite thankful that the male orderly was present. When I examined the patient—as soon

as I walked into the examining room—the patient started complaining of cold chills and hot flushes and wondering why these were present. I'm happy to say that my meetings with the patient as well as with his wife were successful in bringing the patient out of his depression. And I was able to feel myself that I had accomplished something in making the patient more active than he had been—had been at home. And the patient was able to leave after being in the hospital for two weeks. And, essentially, I had been the only person who had been seeing the patient.

Note the many personal pronouns used as subjects of action verbs as well as the paucity of qualifying phrases. These grammatical characteristics of the student's monologue are congruent with her obvious pride in accomplishment.

12. *Passivity.* I have found the most useful verbal reflection of passivity to be the frequent use of the personal pronoun, *me. Me* is almost always used as the object of a verb and therefore is the recipient rather than the initiator of action. Investigation of both normal and deviant speakers has shown that *me* is used significantly more by individuals who are usually thought of as having passive tendencies, that is, small children, elderly people, women, depressive, and compulsive patients (Weintraub, 1981).

The use of *me* to satisfy dependent needs is clearly demonstrated in the example of depressed speech we first encountered on page 67. The reader will recall that the speaker was a hospitalized, middle-aged woman.

13. *Flattery.* Speakers who use flattery in their relationships with others will be found to have high scores in those categories that reflect exaggeration, that is, *evaluators* and *adverbial intensifiers.* In this respect, they are similar to histrionic individuals who are, indeed, frequently flatterers. The following excerpt from a normal woman's monologue illustrates the relationship between flattery and the use of *evaluators* and *adverbial intensifiers*:

> My beautician's name is Carmen. She does a *very nice* cutting job. However, you have to wait a long time when you go in there. And they do a *very good* job on your hair. It's *just* that it's *very confused, especially* on Thursday nights. . . . They all set hair *very nicely.* It's *just* that it's a *shame* to see such *nice* men go to waste. . . . They're *very* high stylish. And they can make your hair look *beautiful.* It's like *wonder.* And they can make it look *so* thick and everything.

14. *Domineering behavior.* This interesting and important personality characteristic has been discussed at length in Chapter 5.

The reader will recall that the most important verbal reflections of domineering speech are commands, verbosity, the use of many connectives (*qualifiers, retractors,* and *explainers*), interruptions, and obscenities.

15. *Creativity.* How can we measure creativity in speech? According to Richard Ohmann (1967), there are only three ways in which creativity can be expressed in language. A writer or speaker can create new words, can make new syntactic associations, that is, put words together in novel ways, and can express himself in original metaphors. The most common way most creative speakers use any or all of these devices is through wit.

The reader may wonder whether verbal creativity in any way reflects other forms of creativity or is simply a characteristic of people with a natural facility for writing or speaking. Although some association between verbal creativity and other forms of originality seems likely, I know of no systematic research on the subject.

16. *Familiarity.* This trait has been extensively discussed in Chapter 5. Its verbal manifestations include the use of first names, questions or comments about the listener's personal life, the mentioning of events or persons conceivably known to the listener but not through shared experiences with the speaker, and so on. *Familiar* individuals frequently use teasing and clowning in their relationships with others, a tactic that many listeners find embarrassing and inappropriate. As we shall see in Chapter 10, Lyndon Johnson was the most *familiar* of the post-World War II Presidents.

17. *Resilience.* This characteristic can be best assessed by measuring the ability of a speaker to lose and then regain his or her verbal style during the course of an interview or, even better, over the course of several interviews spanning days or weeks. A vulnerable speaker may be so traumatized by a failed verbal performance that it will affect his or her ability to respond publicly to questions or even to deliver prepared statements for a time.

18. *Response to Stress.* This characteristic is best measured when the verbal data have been gathered during stress interviews. The speaker's responses to challenging questions are scored and compared with his or her scores when answering more neutral queries. If, for example, a speaker's use of both *qualifiers* and *retractors* increases in response to stress questions, we may conclude that she becomes less decisive, more "waffling" in crisis situations. If, in response to confrontational questions, a speaker uses the pronoun

I more and the pronoun *we* less, it is likely that in crisis situations she will rely more on her own resources and less on help from others. On the other hand, a speaker who cannot accept sole responsibility for crisis decisions is apt to react in the opposite way, by using more *we's* and fewer *I's*.

19. *Autonomy*. Speakers who have a great need for independence from others are often those who keep a tight lid on their feelings (low scores in "emotional" categories) and have a healthy respect for socially defined boundaries (formal behavior in speaking situations, low scores in categories that reflect "engagement" of the listener, such as *direct references* and *rhetorical questions*).

APPLYING VERBAL ANALYSIS TO PRESIDENTIAL INTERVIEWS

In the next chapter, we shall apply our method of personality trait analysis to speech samples of the seven post-World War II U.S. Presidents. I shall rely upon the same source of data I used in the Carter/Reagan study, samples of speech from Presidential news conferences. But, the reader may wonder, why analyze the speech of well-known political leaders? What can possibly be discovered through verbal behavior analysis that cannot be ascertained in more direct ways? Precisely because the reader is already familiar with the personality characteristics of our recent Presidents, our verbal analyses can be compared with what is already known about our Chief Executives. The reader can determine independently if the speech patterns generated by our method reflect Presidential public behavior.

But there is another reason for studying the speech habits of our Presidents. Although this book is neither an historical nor a biographical work, it is, in part, an attempt to develop a method of analysis that may be conceivably useful to investigators of important individuals who are no longer alive. Historians and biographers studying individuals of past eras often must rely on written documents, such as speeches, memoirs, and letters, for much of their raw data. These scholars tend to rely primarily on thematic content to the virtual neglect of grammatical constructions. Character analysis based entirely upon anecdotal data tends to be too impressionistic and fraught with error. Any method that can compare, in a reasonably systematic way, behavior and transcribed speech patterns should be useful to historians and biographers.

SOME PROCEDURAL CONSIDERATIONS

How large a speech sample is necessary for the analysis of a single individual? Under what circumstances should the speech samples be collected? In my experience, a minimum of 5000 words is sufficient for a given speaker. A speaker's verbal samples should be compared only with those of other subjects that have been gathered under similar conditions. Thus, the seven post-World War II Presidents' speech samples we shall be analyzing have all been randomly gathered from news conferences held during the first year in office. Analyzing personality traits requires that the speech samples be gathered under moderately stressful conditions, that is, under conditions that include a certain amount of spontaneity, and, if interviews are used, of confrontation. Since our method is still in an exploratory stage of development, it is important that some independent assessment of the speaker's personality be available for purposes of validation. In the case of the seven post-World War II Presidents, our independent assessment will consist of comments made by historians and biographers who have been neither extreme in their criticism nor unrestrained in their praise of their subjects.

SUMMARY

In this chapter, we have briefly outlined a method of analyzing personality traits of individual speakers. Based partly upon systematic studies of psychiatric populations and partly upon observations gathered during a long clinical career, I have listed the verbal reflections of a number of personality traits that, taken together, give a reasonable picture of a living, functioning human being. It is now time to apply this method to the post-World War II U.S. Presidents.

PART II
The Speaking Styles of Post-World War II U.S. Presidents

CHAPTER 7

Analyzing Presidential News Conferences

Let us now proceed to the analysis of the speaking styles and personalities of U.S. Presidents since World War II. As I have already indicated in the previous chapter, our verbal data consist of Presidential speech samples randomly selected from news conferences held during the first year in office.

PRESIDENTIAL NEWS CONFERENCES AS SOURCES OF BIOGRAPHICAL DATA

Of all the biographical material available to us, why choose Presidential news conferences as the principal data for verbal analysis? The answer is quite simple. Responses to reporters' questions are the only systematically gathered verbal material that are more or less spontaneous and that can be unquestionably attributed to the President. I say "more or less" spontaneous because it is often easy for a President and his advisors to anticipate policy areas in which questions will be asked. A major crisis in foreign affairs, for example, is almost certain to stimulate several questions. Nevertheless, the President cannot know exactly how a question will be phrased or which aspects of a crisis the journalists will choose to emphasize. It is extremely unlikely that the Chief Executive comes with memorized answers to reporters' questions. There is a certain freedom of choice of grammatical structures that may be revealing of personality. Since the President must, to a certain extent, think on his feet, the live news conference permits the public to evaluate his

107

performance under fire. The President's responses to pointed questions constitute a kind of barometer of how he will react in crisis situations. We shall have more to say about the structure of the Presidential news conference later on.

It has been alleged that Presidents are not seriously challenged by live news conferences because they can be briefed for anticipated questions. I disagree. Although some preparation is possible, Presidents and their advisors know the great political opportunities and risks of televised news conferences that are seen by millions of voters. The average viewer cares less about what the President says than about the manner in which he handles himself when jousting with reporters. Few who watched the Nixon-Kennedy debates can recall what subjects were discussed, let alone the exact remarks made by the two candidates. What lingers in the minds of most viewers is the cool, decisive manner of Kennedy compared to the self-conscious, nervous Nixon. Much the same can be said about the Carter-Reagan debates. Before the start of the first debate, Reagan, the challenger, walked across the stage and smilingly shook Carter's hand. Carter appeared surprised and uncomfortable. In my mind, he had already lost the initiative and, probably the debate.

In our previous analyses of public figures, we have shown significant associations between speech patterns and styles of thinking and behaving. The evidence impressively supports a relationship between verbal behavior and personality (Weintraub, 1981). But can such a relationship be said to exist in the case of leaders who carefully tailor their speech habits to accomplish political goals? There is no easy answer to this question. A lot obviously depends upon the degree of spontaneity of the leader's remarks. Psycholinguists generally agree that while it is possible to control the *content* of what one says, grammatical choices are, to a considerable degree, unconsciously determined. Presidential news conferences are reasonably spontaneous for reasons I have already indicated. Since what we are measuring with our method are grammatical choices that are characteristic and not consciously controlled by the speaker, I assume that a President will reveal significant personality traits in answering journalists' questions. As we shall see later on, each President has had his own peculiar way of organizing news conferences, of relating to members of the press, of using opening remarks, and of handling stressful questions. We shall systematically examine each post-World War II President's performance in all of these areas and conclude with a verbal analysis of his speaking style and an attempt to associate with style with significant personality traits. Let us, however, first look at some general aspects of the President's relationship with the press in an era of increasing Presidential power. A survey of the historical development of the Presidential news conference will help us understand why it has become relatively useless as a means of disseminating information but important as a barometer of the President's ability to perform in public.

THE PRESIDENT AND THE PRESS

The importance of the press in the United States has grown as the methods of disseminating news have become more sophisticated and as the power of the Presidency itself has increased. In *The Twilight of the Presidency*, George E. Reedy (1970) wrote: "By the twentieth century, the Presidency had taken on all the regalia of monarchy except robes, a sceptor, and a crown. . . . In time another kingly habit began to appear and Presidents referred to themselves more and more as "we"—the ultimate hallmark of imperial majesty" (p. 22). Reedy went on to describe in great detail all the factors that tend to create an unreal atmosphere in the White House. It is very easy for a protected President to hear only what pleases him from his appointed aides. The office of the Presidency "neither elevates nor degrades a man. What it does is to provide a stage upon which all of his personality traits are magnified and accentuated" (p. 29).

One of the few institutions that does tend to keep the President in touch with reality is the press. Reedy emphasizes that the press tells the President "what he is doing as seen through other eyes . . . a service which . . . will rarely, if ever, be performed by any other medium" (pp. 100–101). Since journalists often play the role of messengers bearing ill tidings, including news that the White House assistants hide from the President, they may be resented by the Chief Executive. Presidential defeats and losses may be attributed to a "hostile" press rather than to errors in judgment. Newspaper criticism may be interpreted as partisan rather than as objective evaluation of Presidential performance. It is only human for Presidents to blame journalists rather than themselves for failed policies.

Presidents have tried to deal with press criticism in several ways. Withholding embarrassing information is one tactic. Often the failure to disclose news of public interest is rationalized on the basis of national security. When the inevitable leaks bring the news items to public attention, the President is apt to accuse the offending reporters of unpatriotic behavior.

Another common method of controlling the press is through intimidation and threats. Franklin D. Roosevelt presented John O'Donnell with an Iron Cross for what he considered to be the journalist's pro-German columns. John F. Kennedy canceled the White House's subscription to the New York *Herald Tribune* in response to criticism of his family.

Those Chief Executives who have enjoyed the best relationships with reporters—Roosevelt, Kennedy, and Reagan—have tried to control the press through seduction. They have carefully cultivated reporters, have made them feel important, and have often been able to win their co-operation despite sharp differences in political ideology. A particular kind of seduction—one that is not without danger—is the Presidential practice of singling out certain reporters for special attention. Favorite journalists who have an "in" with the President are granted exclusive interviews, are leaked important news stories, and are given a certain insight into the President's thinking that is not available to other reporters.

The Role of Television in Shaping Presidential Relationships with Reporters

Television has greatly magnified and modified the relationship between the President and the press. Live Presidential news conferences dramatize the question and answer periods, etching the personalities of President and reporters in the minds of millions of viewers. Because Presidential errors are more significant when made before a huge, live audience, briefings tend to become important. The live Presidential news conference makes performers of the reporters. Previously obscure journalists have become national celebrities thanks to their performance on television. The President has the power to help create a "national image" for a journalist by the way he treats him or her during the news conferences.

Live televised debates and news conferences have become so important in the public mind, that one poor performance can affect a candidate's chances of nomination or election. Reagan's forgetfulness during his first debate with Democratic nominee Mondale in the 1984 Presidential campaign raised the question of his age and competence to lead the country. A similar performance during the second debate might have jeopardized the President's chances of reelection. Fortunately for Reagan, he did better during the second debate, responding with sharpness and humor to Mondale's thrusts. This may have helped return him to the White House.

History of the Presidential News Conference

In his book, *The Imperial Presidency*, Arthur M. Schlesinger, Jr. briefly summarized the history of the Presidential news conference (1973). According to Schlesinger, Theodore Roosevelt was the first President to invite the press into the White House, Woodrow Wilson the first to hold regular press conferences. They were suspended during World War I but were resumed during the 1920s, "under highly circumscribed conditions (pp. 223–228)." Herbert Hoover insisted that all questions be submitted in advance and decided which questions he would or would not answer. Reporters were forbidden to ask follow-up questions and were not allowed to report which questions the President refused to answer. Hoover's news conferences were laconic and dull. He clearly did not enjoy them.

Franklin D. Roosevelt was the originator of the modern press conference. It was he who introduced the informal "give and take" with reporters that his successors have more or less preserved. Roosevelt abolished written questions, and had few limitations on indirect citation, although direct quotations required authorization. During his 12 years in power, he held an average of two press conferences a week. Gregarious and friendly, Roosevelt clearly relished the interaction with reporters and developed the news conference into a powerful instrument of government. As the chief source of governmental news, Roosevelt attracted large numbers of reporters to the Oval Office, where the press conferences were held.

Harry S. Truman reduced the number of news conferences to about one-a-week and held them in the Indian Treaty Room in the old State Department. Whereas the crippled Roosevelt chatted with the reporters while seated at his desk, Truman spoke from a podium.

Dwight D. Eisenhower was the first President to permit news conferences to be taped for television. The first taping was on January 19, 1955. John F. Kennedy went on television live, a practice followed by all subsequent Presidents.

Although the news conference presents the President with an unparalleled opportunity to influence public opinion in his favor, not all Presidents have felt equally at ease answering reporters' questions before a live audience. As we shall see, certain post-World War II Presidents have held very few press conferences. These have usually been the Presidents who have either had an adversarial relationship with the press or whose spontaneous responses to reporters' questions have contained errors of fact or lapses in judgment. Live television broadcasts of news conferences have greatly magnified the significance of Presidential error. Even when there have been no mistakes, a tired or irritable President can severely damage his public image.

Preparing for the Presidential News Conference

George Reedy, a Presidential assistant to Lyndon Johnson, has explained in great detail the structure of the Presidential news conference as well as the extensive preparation necessary for a President to face reporters on live television. Because of the special needs of the television medium and the great expense of television time, "It is usually easier to bring the story to the medium rather than the medium to the story" (Reedy, 1970, p. 155). Prime TV time may become a major issue even in so traditional a presentation as the State of the Union message. The size of the viewing audience takes precedence over other considerations, such as the comfort and convenience of the participants. Tradition is flouted, as it is in professional sports, where the World Series is played on cold October nights in order to attract the largest possible television audience.

Reedy complains that television has drained the Presidential news conference of its spontaneity. He describes a typical live TV press conference in the East Wing of the White House.

> The reporters—in this instance supporting players rather than information seekers—are brought in early to pick their way to a seat through the maze of cords and cables that litter the floor. Their roles are perfectly well understood. They are batting practice pitchers, present to serve the ball up over the plate where the hitter can take a healthy swing. It is accepted practice that the first two questions will be allotted to the wire-service men, and that the traditional "Thank you, Mr. President" will be uttered by the senior wire-service man (p. 155).

The Presidential News Conference as Theater

Reedy goes on to describe what he calls "the show." Because of the demands of television, "the show" must start on time. During a typical press conference, the President will enter the room on cue, usually on the hour or half hour, mount the dais, ask the correspondents to be seated and make his opening remarks. Presidents vary greatly with respect to the regularity with which they make announcements. Certain Presidents, like Nixon and Carter, often went directly to the reporters' questions. Johnson and Kennedy usually had lengthy opening statements to make.

After the opening announcements comes the question and answer period. On either side of the President, according to Reedy, are signal people with "shotgun" microphones that are pointed at the journalists asking the questions. Although the questions are not controlled, the President, Reedy believes, has an easy time of it. The questions are predictable; "follow-up" questions are extremely difficult to ask in such a large gathering (200 to 400 corespondents), and the President has had extensive briefing by his staff prior to the press conference. Reedy complains that "in a process which purports to be the supreme form of communication between a President and his people, the presentation has become the dominant factor. Performance, in a theatrical sense, rides roughshod over the content" (p. 157).

As I have suggested above, Presidential news conferences are not always a breeze. Presidents spend a great deal of time preparing for them and do not always reap political benefits. Certain Presidents have given very few press conferences—Nixon and Reagan are two examples—and for very good reasons. Reporters sometimes *do* ask pointed questions. Nixon was repeatedly and aggressively asked questions about Watergate during certain of his news conferences. The questions clearly irritated him. His responses did not enhance his reputation with the U.S. public.

Reedy's complaint that Presidential news conferences have become theater and have little significant content is certainly true. But they serve a more important purpose than conveying information to the public. News conferences are windows on the President's personality. Reedy is wrong when he states that most of the spontaneity has been drained from the press conferences. Despite the briefings, despite the knowledge that certain questions will be asked, despite all the television trappings designed to make him comfortable, the President is still under considerable stress during meetings with the journalists. Nobody watching Jimmy Carter's labored breathing or Richard Nixon's perspiring performance can doubt that news conferences are anxiety-provoking and do reveal something of the way Presidents respond to stress.

Selecting Presidential News Conference Data

Beginning with the administration of Harry S. Truman, verbatim transcriptions of all Presidential news conferences have been included in the *Public Papers of the Presidents,* which are published annually by the U.S. Government Printing Office. Students of verbal behavior have at their disposal reasonably accurate accounts of Presidential performance under stress, as reflected in spontaneous responses to reporters' questions.

The news conferences contain large amounts of verbal material for each of the Chief Executives. I have limited my analysis of the post-World War II Presidents' speech patterns to the first year in office. For most Presidents, the first year is a "honeymoon" period. Wishing him well and wanting him to succeed, the nation is tolerant of Presidential error and reluctant to direct negative criticism at the Chief Executive. The reporters assigned to the White House reflect this mood to some extent, so that most of the sharp confrontations between the press and the President occur after the first year. We shall, nevertheless, be able to observe marked differences among the Presidents in how they have handled the stress of news conferences.

For each of the seven post-World War II Presidents, I selected 20 samples of 1000 words made up from randomly chosen entries exceeding 30 words. The first sentence of each entry was excluded from the sample. Excluding the first sentence and requiring a minimum of 30 words tends to reduce the effect of dialogue, which is considerable in brief exchanges. I have tried to make the samples of Presidential speech as close to monologues as possible, since this form of discourse allows the fullest display of grammatical structures (Vygotsky, 1962).

In the case of Ronald Reagan, it was not possible to gather 20 samples of 1000 words during his first year in office. For reasons we shall discuss below, Reagan gave only six news conferences, and the question and answer periods were rather short. It was possible to construct only 16 samples of 1000 words for him.

A one-way analysis of variance was performed for the seven Presidents in each of 13 categories. Where significant F-ratios were found, Newman-Keuls tests were done to identify the source of significant differences among the Presidents. The means, standard errors, and significant differences are shown in Figures 7.1–7.4 and Table 7.1.

The results show significant differences in all categories except *retractors.* In a previously published report, however, a Mann-Whitney

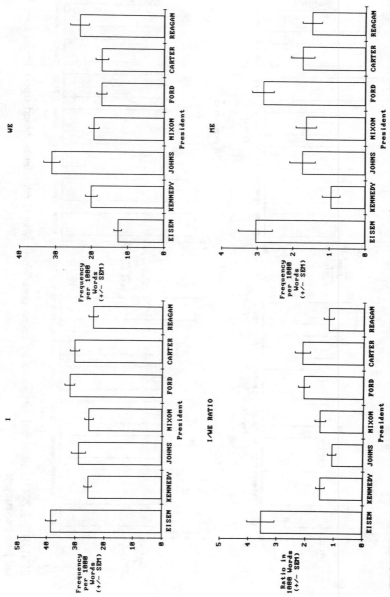

FIGURE 7.1 Use of verbal categories by seven post-World War II presidents, based upon 16-20 speech samples per subject.

115

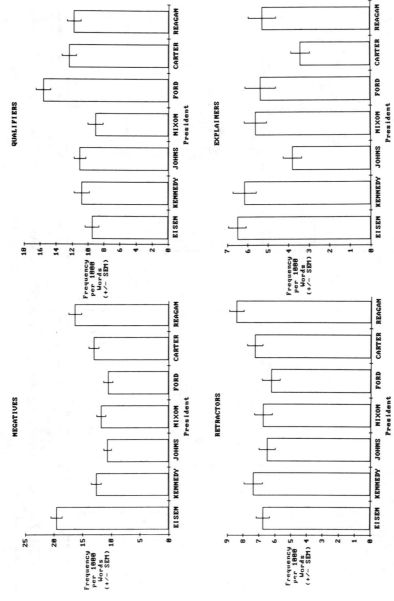

FIGURE 7.2 Use of verbal categories by seven post-World War II presidents, based upon 16–20 speech samples per subject.

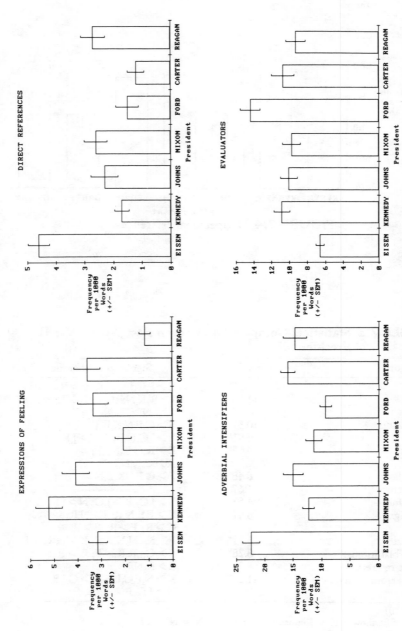

FIGURE 7.3 Use of verbal categories by seven post-World War II presidents, based upon 16–20 speech samples per subject.

117

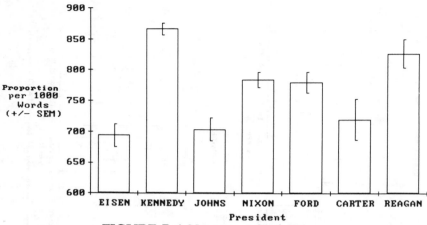

FIGURE 7.4 Nonpersonal references.

TABLE 7.1 Statistical Comparison of Seven Post-World War II Presidents**

Category	F values	Significant differences
I	7.27*	E > F,C,J,K,N,R; F > R
We	11.05*	J > R,K,N,F,C,E; R > E; K > E; N > E
I/we ratio	10.57*	E > C,F,N,K,R,J
Me	4.91*	E > J,C,N,R,K; F > J,K
Negatives	14.65*	E > R,C,K,N,J,F; R > C,K,N,J,F
Qualifiers	6.48*	F > C,R,J,K,E,N
Retractors	1.67	————
Explainers	4.53*	E > J,C; K > J,C; N > C
Feelings	6.47*	K > F,E,N,R; J > N,R; C > R; F > R; E > R
Evaluators	5.71*	F > K,C,J,N,R,E; K > E; C > E
Adverbial intensifiers	8.28*	E > C,J,R,K,N,F; C > F
Direct references	8.88*	E > R,N,J,K,F,C
Nonpersonal references	11.26*	K > N,F,C,J,E; R > C,J,E; N > J,E; F > C,J,E

* p < 0.01
** E = Eisenhower; K = Kennedy; J = Johnson; N = Nixon; F = Ford;
  C = Carter; R = Reagan

U test (Siegel, 1956) revealed a significant difference between the *retractors* scores of Jimmy Carter and Ronald Reagan (Weintraub, 1986).

PRESIDENTIAL PERFORMANCE UNDER STRESS

In Chapter 6, we briefly discussed our strategy for determining a speaker's performance under stressful conditions. The reader will recall that we applied the method of the psychiatric interviewer who creates a minicrisis for the patient by including in the interview several "stress" questions. Based upon the response to these questions, the interviewer can generalize to the patient's probable behavior in crisis situations outside the interviewing room.

In assessing Presidential response to crisis, we shall assume that the question and answer periods are more stressful than the opening remarks period. In comparing the Presidents' use of our verbal categories in the two parts of the press conference, we shall be in a position to note significant shifts in certain directions that may indicate styles of adaptation to stress.

VERBAL BEHAVIOR OF POST-WORLD WAR II U.S. PRESIDENTS

For each President, we shall begin with a brief biographical sketch. The sketch will emphasize personality characteristics, leadership style, and relationships with the press. We shall then proceed to describe the President's manner of addressing the journalists, his way of delivering opening announcements, and some characteristic verbal expressions. Then will come our analysis of the President's verbal behavior during both the opening remarks and the question and answer periods. Using our verbal categories, we shall determine the patterns of grammatical choice and try to see how the President's personality traits are reflected in his speech. We shall discuss the seven post-World War II Presidents in chronological order, beginning with Dwight D. Eisenhower.

CHAPTER 8
Dwight D. Eisenhower

PERSONALITY PROFILE

One of this country's greatest military heroes, Eisenhower was pursued by both major political parties for the 1952 Presidential nomination. Conservative in economic matters and an internationalist in foreign policy, he found the Eastern wing of the Republican Party to be closest to his political views.

Eisenhower's military career prepared him well for the Presidency. According to George Reedy,

> No man who has held the office since George Washington was better equipped to fill the role of the President . . . than Eisenhower. He had dignity . . . warmth . . . obviously a man of good will . . . believed in the validity of America's symbols . . . (had) a touching faith in the capacity of "right reasoning" to solve even the most complex problems . . . a king without arrogance; a potentate with a distaste for power; a moralist with no touch of fanaticism. . . . Nobody could really hate Eisenhower. . . . (Reedy, 1970, pp. 64–65).

Political scientist Neustadt spoke of Eisenhower's ambivalence about the exercise of power. "His confidence was highest when he could assure himself that personal advantage had no place among his aims" (Collier & Horowitz, 1984, p. 252). Schlesinger has attributed Eisenhower's reluctance to concentrate power in the White House to his political philosophy. "Eisenhower had come to the White House as a Whig . . . that is, as one opposed to Presidential usurpation. He believed that Roosevelt and Truman had gathered too much power into the executive branch" (1973, pp. 152–153).

Eisenhower's wish to "preside rather than to rule" did not stem from any lack of self-confidence. In his definitive biography of

Eisenhower, Stephen Ambrose has written, "Eisenhower inspired confidence. . . . He seemed so self-assured, so competent, so open to new ideas and suggestions, so reasonable, so objective" (Ambrose, 1984, p. 17). Eisenhower believed that he was the best qualified person to be President. He did not even defer to the seasoned John Foster Dulles in his conduct of foreign affairs (Ambrose, 1984).

Of his personality traits, honesty and trustworthiness were qualities most often noted in Eisenhower. They were also characteristics that he most valued in himself. Eisenhower could and did lie for his country, however, as in the attempted cover-up of the Gary Powers U-2 flight over Russian territory.

Eisenhower also had a fetish for secrecy that, together with a misplaced trust in the CIA, caused him to make errors (Ambrose, 1984). Another source of mistakes in his defense policies was his faith in the advice of his technical advisors. In certain areas of arms control, he allowed them "to override his own common sense" (p. 621).

LEADERSHIP STYLE

Eisenhower believed in selecting the right people for the right jobs and delegating much of the work to them. He was "free of any need to boost his own ego or to prove his own decisiveness or leadership. . . . (He) wanted to 'build up' the men who worked for him" (Ambrose, 1984, p. 20). He found it "extremely difficult to fire a man who had served him well and loyally, no matter how great a handicap the man had become" (p. 480).

Eisenhower had a great gift for friendship. He chose his friends among a group of wealthy men who would not be likely to abuse their friendship with the President. These friends were always available to Eisenhower when he needed to relax or to get away from the pressures of Washington.

Much has been written about Eisenhower's decision-making methods. What he wanted from his aides was information, "a succinct expression of what his options were" (Ambrose, 1984, p. 509). "He always insisted that every final decision was his as in fact it was" (p. 534).

In general, Eisenhower consulted widely before making important decisions. There were, however, exceptions. One was in certain national defense issues, like nuclear testing, where he felt his own expertise was sufficient. In some other problem areas, his failure to consult others appears to have been due to personal conflict over what policy to pursue. Such conflicts could lead to an inability to act decisively, as in the case of the civil rights demonstrations in the South. It is clear that Eisenhower had little sympathy for the demonstrators. Many of his friends and acquaintances were white Southerners. In deciding civil rights policy, Eisenhower rarely, if ever, consulted with members of minority groups (Ambrose, 1984).

Eisenhower rationalized his failure to act forcefully in behalf of persecuted Americans by narrowly defining the powers of the Presidency and the federal government, particularly in domestic affairs. Such constraints did not apply to his conduct of foreign affairs, where he sometimes pursued aggressive and questionable policies in secret. Two notable examples are the U.S. invasion of Lebanon and the training of Cuban contras for the invasion of Cuba that, under John Kennedy's leadership, led to the disastrous Bay of Pigs adventure.

Eisenhower, above all, wanted to reestablish the dignity of the Presidency. He believed that Truman, his predecessor, had been too crude and partisan a Chief Executive. As President, Eisenhower tried to avoid "mention of any name unless it be done with favorable intent and connotation." He was determined "to reserve all criticism for the private conference" (Ambrose, 1984, p. 164).

Although Eisenhower presided over U.S. fortunes during a period of peace and prosperity, there were numerous crises during his two administrations. His basic strategy for managing them was to deny that they existed. Extremely patient, Eisenhower reacted to surprise events by remaining cool, gathering information, considering his options, and using them to "take control of events" (Ambrose, 1984, p. 354). Speaking and acting with moderation, he waited for passions to cool.

This strategy worked well in foreign policy where his main problem was controlling the hawks of both major political parties. In domestic crises, particularly those requiring aggressive Presidential leadership, Eisenhower's strategy of denial worked less well. By not firmly and forcefully supporting the Supreme Court's desegregation decisions, he allowed Southern whites to believe that they could defy the law with impunity. The racial conflict thus got out of hand and Eisenhower was forced to intervene militarily, an action that might have been prevented had he displayed less ambivalent leadership.

Some have attributed Eisenhower's lack of decisiveness in certain situations to "an exaggerated desire to have everybody happy" (Ambrose, 1984, p. 77). Others have gone further and have accused him of having no convictions he would not compromise. It seems fairer to conclude that Eisenhower procrastinated and compromised when he was in conflict over what course to follow.

Certain of Eisenhower's characteristics were not well-known to the public. He rigidly separated his public from his private life, keeping his Presidential worries from his wife. More than most Presidents, he was able to clear his mind of official business and relax on the golf course or with light reading.

Eisenhower had enormous powers of concentration and could lose himself in his work like few other men. In addition to his difficulties with minority groups, he has been described as uncomfortable with women. Eisenhower also had a hot temper that was well-controlled in public.

Although he was perceived by the public as warm and friendly, Eisenhower avoided physical closeness. Attorney General Brownell was quoted as saying, "Both Eisenhower and [Chief Justice] Warren were very reserved men. If you'd try to put your arm around either of them, he'd remember it for sixty days" (Ambrose, 1984, p. 191).

EISENHOWER AND THE PRESS

As this country's most famous World War II military commander, Eisenhower had a long and positive relationship with the press before assuming the Presidency. He cultivated senior members of the press corps and never allowed their criticism of his performance in office to poison this relationship.

Like most Presidents, Eisenhower wanted to use the press to further his Presidential aims. During World War II, journalists had often been "part of the team, working for the good of the country" (Ambrose, 1984, p. 161). Eisenhower hoped to have this same cooperation from the press as President. He was sensitive to press criticism, particularly when it involved his personal life, but he succeeded in controlling his emotional reactions in public.

EISENHOWER AS SPEAKER AND WRITER

When speaking extemporaneously, Eisenhower's remarks were often poorly organized, grammatically incorrect, and imprecise. Part of the problem was apparently a speech disorder he had had since childhood. He "had always thought faster than he could talk"

(Ambrose, 1984, p. 531), and, as a result, did not always finish his sentences.

Eisenhower made good use of his speaking disability, purposely befuddling the reporters (and his adversaries) when he was not ready to speak out on an issue. Spreading confusion was, in fact, one of his most effective ways of managing a crisis.

If Eisenhower was an indifferent and sloppy speaker, he was a careful writer. Proud of his command of the English language, he is said to have written General Douglas MacArthur's speeches in the 1930s. Eisenhower spent many hours preparing his major speeches and caught mistakes in the drafts that escaped his assistants. In contrast to the careful preparation of his speeches, he only spent about a half-hour with his aides preparing for news conferences.

THE NEWS CONFERENCES OF DWIGHT D. EISENHOWER

Let us now examine the Presidential news conferences held during Eisenhower's first year in office. He met with the press 23 times. All 23 news conferences began with introductory remarks. In general, these opening remarks were brief and informal, rarely exceeding 500 words. When Eisenhower wished to make carefully worded remarks, he read from prepared statements and had copies distributed to the journalists.

The relative lack of preparation of Eisenhower's introductory remarks is clearly reflected by the frequent occurrence of *qualifiers*, which is practically identical to their density during the question and answer periods (about 9 per 1000 words). Unlike most of the other post-World War II Presidents, Eisenhower felt little need to polish his news conference performances. He did not seem to be embarrassed by factual errors or grammatical mistakes. When he didn't know a fact, he asked Press Secretary Hagerty for help. Eisenhower's relaxed, informal style during news conferences reflected the self-confidence he felt with the reporters. He had no need to impress them or the American people with his cleverness or speaking style.

Eisenhower's determination to restore dignity to the White House was reflected in his behavior with the reporters. He was friendly but quite reserved. Although the journalists were asked, at the beginning of the first press conference, to identify themselves by name when asking questions, Eisenhower often did not use their names when addressing them. When he did, it was almost always as

"Mr.," "Miss," or "Mrs." When addressing the reporters as a group, it was usually as "Ladies and Gentlemen."

Some Favorite Expressions

Like most speakers, Eisenhower had his favorite words and expressions, such as "a little bit," "you might say," "I do believe," and so on. What most distinguished Eisenhower's choice of words, however, was his lavish use of adverbs, particularly *adverbial intensifiers*. Both opening remarks and answers to questions were punctuated with adverbs like "properly," "merely," "terrifically," "very," and "quite." As we shall see, the high frequency of *adverbial intensifiers* was partly responsible for Eisenhower's perceived warmth.

Eisenhower's Humor

Eisenhower's press conferences were serious and relatively free of humor. The President did not tell many jokes, so that any attempt at humor, no matter how feeble, was able to get laughs from the press corps. He showed great patience with the journalists. Eisenhower was calm, never lost his temper, and always treated reporters with respect. He never made jokes at their expense.

Verbal Analysis

Eisenhower differed from other Presidents in a number of interesting ways. He made the most frequent use of the pronoun *I* and the least use of the pronoun *we*. His discussions of national and international issues were highly personal; Eisenhower frequently referred to wartime experiences when illustrating a point. He rarely used the imperial *we*. Such a practice would have violated his concept of a Presidency with limited authority.

There may be other reasons for Eisenhower's frequent use of the pronoun *I*. He did not arrive at decisions through consensus. Assignments were delegated to subordinates who presented the President with alternatives when decisions had to be made. Important decisions were *I*, not *we* judgments.

Another factor contributing to the high *I/we* ratio may have been Eisenhower's unique position in the Republican Party. He was no ordinary leader. A great and popular war hero, Eisenhower was approached by many influential Republicans as the candidate who could lead them to the White House after 20 years of Democratic incumbency. He did not have to come to them. This enviable position of being above ordinary party politics may have contributed to Eisenhower's sense of personal ownership of the White House.

Eisenhower's Warmth Reflected in His Grammatical Choices

Much of Eisenhower's popularity can be attributed to his personal warmth. Dignified and reserved, he nevertheless communicated a sense of concern and caring to the American people. How were these traits reflected in his grammatical choices? The reader will recall our principal "emotional" categories: *expressions of feeling, adverbial intensifiers, evaluators, nonpersonal references, direct references,* and the *I/we ratio.*

Eisenhower's scores in the "feelings" categories make him the most emotional of the post-World War II Presidents. The only expressive category in which he was not on the emotional side is *evaluators.* In four "feelings" categories, his scores are the highest of all the Presidents (*I/we ratio, personal references, adverbial intensifiers,* and *direct references*).

It comes as something of a surprise to learn that Eisenhower scored high in *adverbial intensifiers,* a category usually associated with histrionic behavior. His frequent use of adverbs is illustrated in the following answer to a reporter's question:

> I know *only* about the first part of the statement you make—in other words, your premise, which is that up to this moment the cost of the Korean war has *never* been *really* budgeted. There has *merely* been an expression of hope that it would be over *soon.* Now, *just exactly* how the Defense Department and the Bureau of the Budget expect to come up with a plan for correcting that, I am not sure, so I couldn't comment (Public Papers of the Presidents of the United States, 1960, p. 133).

Eisenhower's moderate use of *qualifiers* and *retractors* suggests an ability to make decisions and to stick to them. There is no evidence in his grammatical choices of either paralysis of decision or impulsivity. This finding is, in general, congruent with what we know of Eisenhower from biographical sources.

Oppositional Behavior an Important Eisenhower Trait

In some ways, the most interesting finding in Eisenhower's scores is an extremely high occurrence of *negatives.* Of the other post-

World War II Presidents, only Ronald Reagan comes close to Eisenhower in this category. Over the years, I have come to interpret high levels of *negatives* in two ways. On the surface, *negatives* seem to represent a stubborn, oppositional streak in the speaker. When pushed, such a speaker refuses to budge, becomes less rather than more compliant. On a deeper level, a high *negatives* score may indicate a tendency to deny, a disinclination to look at unpleasant realities if they dictate actions that are difficult for the speaker.

Eisenhower certainly had a combative streak, although he tried to conceal it from the public. It is a tribute to his self-discipline and political skill that he was able successfully to hide this less attractive aspect of his personality from an admiring public.

Not wishing to look at unpleasant realities was most noticeable in Eisenhower's handling of the excesses of Senator Joseph McCarthy. Reluctant to take action or to speak out against a fellow Republican whose anti-Communist views he shared, he closed his eyes to McCarthy's highly destructive activities and allowed many innocent citizens, including U.S. Army personnel, to be hurt.

Comparing Eisenhower's Opening Remarks and His Replies to Questions

We have already noted that Eisenhower did not carefully prepare the opening remarks of his news conferences. His announcements contained as many qualifying phrases as did his answers to reporters' questions. With respect to Eisenhower's use of other verbal categories, the main difference was in the much greater frequency of *negatives* during the question and answer periods. We can conclude from this finding that under stress Eisenhower showed oppositional behavior and, perhaps, a refusal to face unpleasant facts. No great harm resulted when inaction was the strategy of choice, as was often the case during the Eisenhower Presidency. In controversial matters requiring action, Eisenhower's disinclination to deal with disagreeable issues proved costly to the nation.

Befuddling the Press and the Nation

Eisenhower's speaking difficulties, and his grammatical errors in particular, have been noted. He used this disability to purposely confuse reporters when he did not want to give a straightforward answer. Confusing answers were common when he was asked about the activities of Senator Joseph McCarthy. Consider the following exchange, taken from the question and answer period of Eisenhower's April 22, 1953, press conference. It concerned an attempt by Senator McCarthy to organize a boycott of Communist bloc countries by Greek shipowners. McCarthy's action raised the question of legislative interference in the President's conduct of foreign policy.

RICHARD L. WILSON
    (Cowles Publications): Mr. President, would you agree that Senator McCarthy's actions on the Greek ship matter had undermined administrative policy?
PRESIDENT EISENHOWER: You have asked a question, of course, that is one of opinion; many people can have different kinds of answers. I think not, because I think there is sufficient power in the Secretary of State, and in the Presidency, to remind all peoples—others, and including our own—that the exclusive power of negotiating such arrangements, anything that is legal, belongs to the Executive, and comes into being when two-thirds of the Senate ratify. So I doubt that an action—even, let us say, that we would agree it was misguided; if that were so, I doubt that act can undermine the prestige and the power that resides in the Government and in its various parts as viewed by the Constitution (Public Papers of the Presidents of the United States, 1960, p. 149).

    Eisenhower's answer to the reporter's question was typical of his handling of crisis situations. By refusing to recognize that an unpleasant or dangerous situation existed, he succeeded in soothing feelings and avoiding an escalation of rhetoric. Usually, this strategy worked. Sometimes, as in the case of McCarthy, it didn't. Finally, it was Congress that took the initiative in curbing the activities of the Wisconsin Senator. Eisenhower's view of the proper role of the President was supportive of Congressional rather than Presidential action. Until the end, he refused to see the behavior of McCarthy as anything more than an internal problem of the legislature.

SUMMARY

Eisenhower's speech pattern suggests a highly confident leader who was relatively unconcerned with his performance at news conferences. Generally able to make decisions and stick to them, Eisenhower could become indecisive in policy areas where the national interest and personal inclinations clashed. Oppositional when challenged, he was able to personally engage his critics and express his opinions in an emotionally forceful way. Eisenhower's lavish use of "feelings" categories makes him the warmest of our post-World War II Presidents, a quality that was partly responsible for his great popularity.

Eisenhower's modest comportment in public hid a healthy and robust ego. In private conversations, he considered himself the most qualified American to be President. In no way did he regard himself as an accident of history. There were times when he came close to considering himself indispensable and was contemptuous of most of his rivals. Dominant, well-informed, and in control of important decisions, Eisenhower, for political reasons, might allow the public to believe that he was following the lead of a powerful subordinate like Secretary of State John Foster Dulles. It is now clear that Eisenhower carefully orchestrated both foreign and domestic policy while displaying to the public a facade of relaxation and good humor.

CHAPTER 9

John F. Kennedy

PERSONALITY PROFILE

Raised in a family preoccupied with politics, success, and image, John Kennedy's personality and career reflect a blending of these three obsessions. After the death of older brother Joe in World War II, the mantle of political ambition passed to John. Although lacking the aggressiveness and physical strength of his older brother, John did not lack for self-confidence. Observers of the former President agree that he was physically courageous and active, although not to the same degree as some of the other Kennedys (Collier and Horowitz, 1984). Indeed, John was the most bookish of the Kennedys, the only one of the family who "looked things up" (pp. 64–66). Although proud of his literary interests and accomplishments, Kennedy preferred to project a "macho" rather than an intellectual image.

Kennedy possessed to a remarkable degree the qualities of detachment and irony. Competing with a physically stronger older brother, he "was forced to resort to the skills of the weak—speed and cunning" (Collier and Horowitz, 1984, p. 61). His primary weapon in interpersonal combat was verbal. His irony and sarcasm were at once a source of his charm and occasions for offending people.

Since the family's ambitions for political success focused for so many years on brother Joe, John was able to enjoy, to a greater extent than Joe, the pleasures of childhood. Until his death, he retained a certain boyishness that was enormously appealing to the public. He has been called a Peter Pan, "an American Prince Hal" (Collier and Horowitz, 1984, p. 148).

Like most Kennedys, John was preoccupied with impressions,

with how he was seen and judged by others. The family's involvement with Hollywood brought him into contact with glamorous movie stars, who fascinated him. He is said to have moved into his role of politician "like a method actor. . . . Hollywood stars fascinated him. . . . They embodied what he was and what he wanted to become" (Collier and Horowitz, 1984, pp. 234–236). More than any other U.S. President, Kennedy came close to being a charismatic leading man, combining "the best qualities of Elvis Presley and Franklin D. Roosevelt" (White, 1961, p. 396).

Curiosity and a practical cast of mind are two traits that Kennedy possessed to an extreme. Free of a clearly defined ideology, neither a liberal nor a conservative, relatively untouched by the trauma of the Great Depression, he never developed a coherent program around which his supporters could rally. On the other hand, not being bound to any political orthodoxy enabled him to be flexible under fire (Kearns-Goodwin, 1987).

LEADERSHIP STYLE

Getting America moving was certainly an idea that came naturally to a kinetic Kennedy. He wanted very much to be a strong President but respected the prerogatives of the other branches of government, particularly the Congress. He was unwilling or unable to use the manipulative methods of a Lyndon Johnson, and his programs suffered in Congress as a result.

Kennedy possessed a peculiar combination of courage and caution. He is quoted as having said, "I intend to be as brave as I dare." He was "pragmatic, testing the limits, but not getting caught on any limb of commitment that might be sawed off from behind" (Collier and Horowitz, 1984, pp. 234–236).

As a leader, Kennedy often circumvented established administrative bodies such as the cabinet, relying on the more flexible National Security Council or on ad hoc committees "composed of officials in whose judgment he had . . . confidence" (Reedy, 1970, p. 77). After the Bay of Pigs disaster, Kennedy depended more and more on his brother, Robert, believing that in moments of crisis only a family member could be fully trusted.

Normally disciplined and controlled, Kennedy was reckless and foolish in his relationships with women. Handsome, charming, and witty, he was enormously attractive to women and became sexually involved with a great number of them both before and during his marriage. His many liaisons continued into the Presidency but were successfully hidden from the public until after his assassination. Described as a romantic, in the Byronic tradition, Kennedy was apparently more interested in the pursuit and conquest of women than in being close to them (Collier and Horowitz, 1984; Kearns-Goodwin, 1987).

Kennedy has been described as intolerant of interpersonal stress and could not stand people sulking in his presence (Collier and Horowitz, 1984). He was quite different in handling the more impersonal crises of public life, in which he was invariably calm, cool, and dignified. He tried to master stressful situations by anticipation and careful preparation. He behaved in any crisis "as if it consisted only of a sequence of necessary things to be done that (would) become complicated if emotions intruded" (White, 1961, p. 340). In private conversations, Kennedy was known to express anxiety in a variety of nonverbal ways. "(He) flutters his hands, he adjusts his necktie, slaps his knee, strokes his face." Under public scrutiny, as in the Nixon debates, Kennedy was "calm and nerveless in appearance" (White, 1961, p. 346). Nor could he be provoked into public displays of temper. When angry, he was "at his most precise, almost schoolmasterish" (White, 1961, p. 177). Kennedy subscribed to the notion that revenge is better than anger. And, indeed, he was a man "who never forgot either friend or enemy" (White, 1961, p. 5).

KENNEDY AND THE PRESS

Throughout his public life, Kennedy enjoyed a positive and close relationship with members of the press. To begin with, he liked and respected journalists. A one-time reporter and Pulitzer Prize winner, he was a compulsive reader. He enjoyed good writing; ideas were extremely important to him (White, 1961). Kennedy realized the importance of the press for his political ambitions, particularly for an outsider like himself, and consciously set about seducing reporters. He religiously read press dispatches, complimenting journalists if he liked what they wrote. He made himself and his aides available to the press during his busy campaign schedules (White, 1961). He would ask newspeople for their advice, flattered them, and tried to make their job easier. As a result, reporters covering the Presidential campaign clearly preferred to travel with Kennedy than with the more withdrawn and suspicious Nixon. It is a matter of record that the press protected Kennedy by keeping from the public aspects of his personal life that contradicted the carefully cultivated image of a clean-cut, strong Catholic family man.

Kennedy not only rewarded favorable news reporting of his candidacy and Presidency, he actively tried to suppress unfavorable news, an old family habit. Fascinated by publicity and image-making, Kennedy was the first President "to see the full possibilities of TV as a medium of self-promotion" (Collier and Horowitz, 1984, p. 280).

THE NEWS CONFERENCES OF JOHN F. KENNEDY

During the first year in office, Kennedy held 19 formal press conferences. With the exception of the final news conference on November 29, 1961, all meetings with the journalists began with opening announcements. The frequency of *qualifiers* in Kennedy's opening remarks was 2.9 per 1000 words, indicating careful preparation.

The tone of Kennedy's press conferences was formal and impersonal. He rarely referred to a reporter by name, although he knew many of them very well. Whereas Eisenhower's responses to questions were usually brief, rarely exceeding 200 words, Kennedy often spoke at great length; some of his responses were more than 400 words.

Praised as "one of the more gifted conversationalists of politics" (White, 1961, p. 65), Kennedy's answers to reporters' questions were cogent and lucid. When he wished to avoid part of a question, he simply did not refer to it in his reply rather than try to confuse the journalists as Eisenhower did. Although generally free of grammatical error, Kennedy often allowed his sentences to run on to exhausting lengths. Consider the following example from his February 1 news conference (Public Papers of the Presidents of the United States, 1962, p. 33).

> I'm not a candidate for office for at least 4 years, so that there will be many ups and downs I suppose during that period, so that anybody who thinks that if things get better in the spring that we'll be able to say that they're the result of the administration policy and that's the reason that I painted them unnecessarily dark, misunderstands completely.

Kennedy was well-controlled during his news conferences. Reserved and polite, he did not allow himself to be provoked into displays of irritation or anger. Kennedy did not respond defensively to pointed comments and, when he could, defused confrontational questions with humorous replies. These subtle, ironic rejoinders contributed a great deal to his charm and effectiveness with reporters. His wit tended to be self-depreciating and never at the journalists' expense. Kennedy always treated his inquisitors with great respect, and this helps account for the esteem in which they held him. The following excerpt (speaking about the possibility of some of his legislation dying in the House Rules Committee) is typical of Kennedy's press conference humor:

> Shouldn't the Members of the House themselves and not merely the members of the Rules Committee have a chance to vote on those measures? But the responsibility rests with the Members of the House, and I would not attempt in any way to infringe upon that responsibility. I merely give my view as an interested citizen (Laughter). Public Papers of the Presidents of the United States, 1962, p. 11).

Favorite Words and Expressions

"Judgment" was one of Kennedy's favorite words. He used it to mean either "opinion," i.e., "It is a judgment as to what is the best use to make of the funds that are available" (Public Papers of the Presidents of the United States, 1962, p. 10) or "decision," i.e., "We will come . . . to some judgment as to whether a more satisfactory method of protecting our gold could be secured. . . ." (p. 13). Other favorite Kennedy words and expressions were "concern," "useful" or "usefully," "I am hopeful," and "in my opinion." He often spoke of his administration or the nation being "tested" in the years ahead.

In order to increase the force of an opinion or judgment, Kennedy would frequently use the auxiliary word "do," i.e., "I *do* think, "I *do* believe." I have already referred to the great length of many of his sentences. They would often contain embedded phrases and clauses.

Verbal Analysis

Kennedy's detachment is well revealed in his choice of grammatical structures. Of the seven Presidents, he had the highest *nonpersonal references* score. With one exception, he did not score high in any category associated with emotion. That one exception, *expressions of feeling*, may be only apparent. Kennedy's high score is due almost entirely to his use of "low voltage" expressions such as "I am hopeful" or "I am glad," and so on.

What else does Kennedy's speech pattern reveal? His moderate *qualifiers* and *retractors* scores indicate an ability to make decisions and to reconsider choices already made. There is no evidence of impulsivity in Kennedy's speech. A low *me* score—the lowest of all the Presidents—speaks against a passive streak, and a modest *adverbial intensifiers* score reflects a subdued rather than an overt theatrical style.

Kennedy's *negatives* score was moderate, suggesting an ability to say "No" without being stubborn. He was apparently able to look facts in the face even when they were unpleasant. There is no evidence of strong denial tendencies.

Like Eisenhower, Kennedy enjoyed meeting the press and held many news conferences during his first year in office. He performed well and seemed comfortable on live television. Part of Kennedy's ease came from his careful preparation. We know that he reviewed anticipated questions with his aides before the news conferences. Possessed of an excellent memory and well-developed verbal skills, Kennedy was able to answer most questions intelligently and at great length.

Kennedy's Response to Interview Stress

How did Kennedy respond to stress questions? He was given neither to impulsive nor to angry replies. Kennedy did not try to deny unpleasant allegations. What he did was either ignore a difficult question, answer around it, or simply repeat his version of the facts. Unexpected stress questions could, in these ways, be filed away for additional thought and consultation.

During his many press conferences, Kennedy revealed almost nothing of his personal life. His family was well protected from the curiosity of the press corps.

SUMMARY

Articulate, witty, well-informed and prepared, President Kennedy obviously enjoyed meeting with journalists. Although personally acquainted with many of the reporters, he scrupulously avoided showing signs of shared knowledge and experience during the news conferences. At all times, Kennedy was dignified, formal, reserved, and respectful. He did not respond defensively to pointed questions nor did he show hostility toward reporters. His humor was subtle, ironic, and self-depreciating.

Kennedy held 19 rather long news conferences during his first year in office. There were extensive opening remarks that were carefully prepared and wordy answers to reporters' questions. Kennedy's sentences were sometimes run-on and might contain embedded clauses and phrases, suggesting an ability to consider complex issues or a difficulty in containing a rush of thoughts.

Kennedy made little use of "emotional" verbal categories. This enhanced the impression of a cool, detached leader thoroughly in command of the situation.

A moderate use of *qualifiers* and *retractors* reflects the personality of a leader who could make decisions and reconsider them without yielding to impulse. A moderate *negatives* score suggests that Kennedy was not oppositional or stubborn and approached questions of state in a positive way. Although wishing to be a strong President, Kennedy, like Eisenhower, did not often use the "imperial" we. His use of the pronouns, *I*, *we*, and *me* reflects a healthy ego, an ability to work with others, and an absence of strong passive strivings.

When stressed by difficult questions or surprised by unexpected ones, Kennedy either ignored them or tried to turn them aside with witty rejoinders. He did not attempt impulsive answers when unprepared. Preparation and control were extremely important to him and to the public image he was trying to project to the American people. Kennedy did not resort to Eisenhower's practice of calling upon his aides to provide him with facts during a news conference.

Based upon his news conference behavior, it is reasonable to assume that Kennedy's way of handling crises was to keep calm and cool and to try to buy time until further thought and consultation allowed for an informed decision to be made.

CHAPTER 10
Lyndon B. Johnson

INTRODUCTION

Enormously ambitious for the Presidency, Lyndon B. Johnson could become Chief Executive only through the death of John F. Kennedy. An extraordinarily competent senator, Johnson was considered to be too provincial in manner and speech to win the Presidency on his own. As President he was most effective during the transitional years between the Kennedy assassination and his own election to the Presidency in 1964.

Johnson was the perfect leader to calm the distraught nation, achieve consensus between the two parties, and guide the Kennedy legislative program through Congress. Never as comfortable in foreign as in domestic affairs, Johnson finally came to grief in his handling of the Vietnam war and the antiwar movement in the United States. The narrowness of his vision as well as certain personality flaws led inexorably to his fall from public favor and his subsequent decision not to be a candidate for reelection to the Presidency.

PERSONALITY PROFILE

As in our treatment of all the post-World War II Presidents, we shall limit ourselves to those aspects of Johnson's personality about which there is general agreement. Observers of Johnson have noted his enormous physical vigor. His capacity for work was prodigious (White, 1965). He drove his staff as mercilessly as he drove himself. He has been described as having a cruel streak toward those who worked for him when they did not perform up to his extremely high standards (White, 1965).

Extraordinarily gregarious, Johnson cultivated anyone who could be of use to him. He had an enormous number of colleagues but few close friends (White, 1965). He could not tolerate being alone. A workaholic, Johnson had trouble relaxing (Reedy, 1970).

Johnson loved to give to people but he expected gratitude from those he helped. Yet he was not a vindictive person. Johnson was able to work effectively with people who had previously offended him.

One of Johnson's traits was love of attention. Sensitive to criticism, he found indifference unforgivable. Obsessed with himself and his performance, Johnson would doze off when he could not dominate a conversation (White, 1965).

He was very self-conscious about his Texas hill country origins and occasionally showed it by embarrassing Eastern visitors with his coarse humor. He was deeply hurt when his rural Texas style was criticized in the press.

No politician was more sensitive to the needs and desires of others and Johnson used this perspicacity to further his political career. He possessed a great number of personae, which he skillfully exhibited to different audiences and on different occasions.

We have already referred to Johnson's extremes of cruelty and kindness. His biographers note other polarities in his character. He displayed "the most extreme swings between tenderness and cruelty, between dedication and cynicism, between comedy and high purpose" (White, 1965, p. 344).

One of our more loquacious Presidents, Johnson was a great raconteur. "He could, to great effect, convincingly appear to recreate the look and feel of any person in almost any situation, whether he himself had been there or not. . . . Ribbing and teasing . . . were central to all Johnson stories. By directing his ridicule toward someone outside the assembled group, he created an atmosphere of intimacy inside, a feeling of camaraderie" (Kearns, 1976, pp. 8–9).

LEADERSHIP STYLE

Lyndon B. Johnson has been described as "a man without an ideology" (White, 1965, p. 477). Ill at ease with subtle political philosophies and abstractions, Johnson functioned best when dealing with concrete problems requiring specific solutions.

Johnson disliked confrontation and was uncomfortable fighting enemies directly. He tried to achieve consensus by building alliances based upon mutual interest. According to Schlesinger, Johnson's need for consensus "was a matter of psychological need as well as of political strategy" (1973, p. 185).

Accused of trying to establish an "imperial" Presidency, Johnson held "an old and honest belief in the spacious Presidential authority to deploy force abroad" (Schlesinger, 1973, p. 177). In Johnson's view, the role of Congress "was not to sanction but to support the [Vietnam] War" (Schlesinger, 1973, p. 181).

Johnson's handling of day-to-day matters was diametrically opposed in style to that of Eisenhower. The reader will recall that Eisenhower delegated the details of government to subordinates and wished to have alternatives brought to him for final decisions. Johnson liked to keep control of the smallest details (Reedy, 1970). This is not surprising. He had succeeded in obtaining power throughout his career by meticulous attention to detail, by seeing opportunity in the most menial assignments, by exploiting ambiguous rules, by catering to the often overlooked but psychologically important desires of people he wanted to cultivate.

Although Johnson appears to have had a chameleon's ability to present himself in the most varied ways to different people, he was much more than an expedient politician bent on obtaining and exercising power. He had a genuine and passionate desire to help the poor and minorities and to achieve a more equitable distribution of wealth in the United States by increasing opportunity for those groups that lacked it.

In foreign policy, Johnson assumed that leaders of other countries could be managed in the same way as U.S. senators. He was convinced by his World War II experiences that firmness in dealing with our enemies would prevent the kind of worldwide conflagration that followed the appeasement of Hitler. Johnson was unprepared to deal with the subleties of the Vietnam war.

JOHNSON'S HANDLING OF
CRISIS SITUATIONS

Johnson's behavior in crisis situations depended to a great extent on the nature of the crisis and the kind of response it called for. When Presidential behavior called for gathering a consensus to reach certain specific goals that Johnson could understand, he was at his best. His management of the transitional problems following the assassination of John F. Kennedy was magnificent. Much the same can be said of his handling of civil rights issues. His intuitive grasp of the political possibilities of civil rights progress in the aftermath of the Kennedy assassination allowed him to use the kind of persuasion, for which he was justly celebrated, to guide landmark legislation through Congress.

Crisis situations involving Johnson's own future posed more serious problems for him. Running for office meant facing voter rejection. Johnson often became ill when pursuing political office (Kearns, 1976). Fears of defeat made every questionable race a crisis for him and he was often tempted to withdraw. This reaction accounts, in part, for Johnson's withdrawal from the 1968 Presidential campaign at a rather early stage of the struggle. It is not at all clear that Johnson could not have pulled things out as Truman had. He certainly could have had the nomination had he wanted it and Nixon was far from being a certain winner.

It was the Vietnam War that undid Johnson. He clearly did not understand the issues, and was helpless in a situation where he could not buy off an implacable enemy or unsympathetic allies. His tendency to divide foreign leaders into "good" and "bad" and into "helpful" and "not helpful," his inability to understand that foreign peoples might be motivated by factors other than an acquisition of material comforts rendered Johnson's wheeling and dealing style unsuitable to the handling of the Vietnam crisis. A further complication was his inability to listen to people who disagreed with his policy. It was in this fatal crisis that Johnson demonstrated that conversing with others was always to convince, not to be convinced (Schlesinger, 1973).

JOHNSON'S RELATIONSHIP WITH THE PRESS

Johnson greatly respected the power of the press. He believed that without the support of the media no President could lead effectively for very long (Kearns, 1976). Journalists were approached like members of any other special interest group. Johnson believed that reporters had their own constituencies—their editors and publishers or some group of readers they wanted to please. The way to get good coverage was to discover who these private constituents were and then "control the strings to the private story" behind the public story (Kearns, 1976, p. 247).

According to Kearns, during Johnson's tenure as majority leader of the Senate, Johnson's methods were quite successful with the

Senate press corps. They needed the majority leader because there were few other sources of information. "This was less true in the White House, where correspondents could obtain information from other sources: from members of the White House staff, from the agencies and from the Congress. Prior experience with a number of submissive correspondents led Johnson to the erroneous conclusion that his press relations could be solved by the art of seduction" (Kearns, 1976, p. 303).

LYNDON B. JOHNSON'S PRESS CONFERENCES

During the first 13 months of his Presidency, Johnson held 35 news conferences, the most of any post-World War II President. As a rule, a President's ease with the press is reflected by the number of press conferences he gives. Presidents with good press relations will expose themselves to journalists' questions more frequently than those with poor rapport.

Johnson was an exception to this rule. Although his relations with the press corps were not particularly good, he held frequent press conferences. They were managed, however, in such a way, that he was able to control their content and direction. Unwilling to face the discomfort and embarrassment of answering difficult questions, he avoided regularly scheduled meetings with the press corps. His news conferences were often announced at the last minute and generally held on weekends. "The frequency of [Johnson's] press conferences varied with his changes of mood; when he felt good, he would hold four or five conferences within a few weeks; when he felt persecuted, he could go for months without any conferences at all" (Kearns, 1976, p. 248). Most of Johnson's news conferences were brief. They often began with extensive opening remarks, leaving little time for questions.

Not only were Johnson's press conferences called without extensive notice and at inconvenient times, they were frequently held in cramped quarters. This created a charged atmosphere that occasionally led to irritable exchanges, as in the January 25, 1964 press conference:

REPORTER: Are you going to have the press conference in this office or the State Department?
PRESIDENT: I don't know where we will have it. I think it is good enough to say I'm going to have one. (Public Papers of the Presidents of the United States, 1965, pp. 232–233).

Johnson's press conferences were the most informal of the post-World War II Presidents. Consider the way he began his first news conference on December 7, 1963:

> THE PRESIDENT: I told [Press Secretary] Pierre [Salinger] a little earlier in the morning I was going to buy coffee later in the day, and I didn't really know how much coffee I was going to buy. He has more friends than I anticipated (Public Papers of the Presidents of the United States, 1965, p. 34).

Johnson's Domination of the Press

Lyndon Johnson's domineering personality was evident in a variety of ways. We have already referred to his practice of keeping reporters off balance by announcing the time and place of news conferences at the last moment. Another Johnson tactic was to be extremely curt when in a bad mood or when asked questions he didn't want to answer, as in the following example from the March 21, 1964 news conference. The President had opened the meeting by reading a statement to the President of the Organization of American States relative to the United States dispute with Panama. The exchange took place later in the news conference:

> REPORTER: Mr. President, what is the reason for issuing the statement today?
>
> THE PRESIDENT: No reason. I am sending it over there. I didn't think you would object to hearing it.
>
> REPORTER: No, I meant—I mean to the OAS. What is the reason for sending the statement to them now?
>
> THE PRESIDENT: So that we may reiterate our viewpoint and in some detail.
>
> REPORTER: Mr. President, would you think that this statement might clear up any difference of interpretation they have—
>
> THE PRESIDENT: [interrupts] I would not speculate on that. (Public Papers of the Presidents of the United States, 1965, p. 406).

In addition to the brevity of some of Johnson's responses and the interruptions, the reader will note the extreme sensitivity to perceived criticism of his actions.

A leader of striking contrasts, Johnson went from the extreme of giving curt responses to unwelcome questions to providing the longest answers of any post-World War II President to questions he *did* want to answer. Some of Johnson's answers exceeded 1000 words (about 10 minutes) without interruption.

Preparation of Opening Remarks

Johnson's opening remarks included both off-the-cuff statements and carefully planned announcements that he read to the journalists. He used about 3.5 qualifying phrases per 1000 words, which suggests systematic preparation. Johnson was most effective in one-on-one conversations and did not enjoy public discussions of issues. Press conferences are hard to control and he dreaded appearing foolish or unprepared (Kearns, 1976).

Johnson as "Imperial President"

Of all the post-World War II Presidents, Lyndon B. Johnson was most given to the use of the "imperial" *we*, a habit generally assumed by kings and emperors. Consider this excerpt from Johnson's first news conference on December 7, 1963 (Public Papers of the Presidents of the United States, 1965, p. 35).

THE PRESIDENT: We think we have made very good progress in showing the continuity in our transition. We have tried to, second, give a sense of unity in the country and in the world. We have met the leaders, some 90 of them from the various nations in the world.

Not infrequently, Johnson used another "imperial" device, referring to himself in the third person, as "the President." During the December 18, 1963, press conference, he responded as follows to a question about the budget:

THE PRESIDENT: No one knows what the budget will be now, because we are trying the case, so to speak. We have dozens of agencies, independent agencies and Cabinet departments, who have made their requests and have not yet had it acted upon. Once it is acted upon, they still have the right to appeal to *the President*. The Joint Chiefs will appeal to *the President* from the recommendations they have made on December 30th at Johnson City (Public Papers of the Presidents of the United States, 1965, p. 66).

Johnson's Press Conference Humor

The tone of most of Johnson's news conferences was quite serious. When in a good mood, he would occasionally make joking remarks. They usually took the form of teasing his aides, as in the following excerpt from the December 26, 1963 news conference (Public Papers of the Presidents of the United States, 1965, p. 88).

THE PRESIDENT: [An] observation I want to make is that I gave [Press Secretary] Pierre [Salinger] that jacket he has on today because it is too large for me to wear—or too small.

Johnson was much more likely to be light and informal during news conferences held in Texas. During appearances before national televised audiences, he was extremely serious and formal, because of his fear of appearing provincial and undignified (Reedy, 1970).

Favorite Words and Expressions

When dealing with budgetary matters, Johnson would pepper his remarks with a number of "money saving" expressions. He would not act "wastefully," he did not intend to "waste a dime," he intended to get "a dollar's value for a dollar spent." On the other hand, when pushing for expensive programs, he didn't "want to just be a tightwad." Johnson used many "consensus" expressions. At a time during which he was trying ruthlessly to manipulate the White House press corps, he spoke of arranging news conferences "with your counsel and cooperation." While exerting enormous pressure on Congress to pass his legislative program, he publicly emphasized the need for Congress to make its own decisions "in their wisdom." Johnson sought "areas of agreement," expressed his willingness to discuss "anything, anytime, anywhere" with "men and women of good will."

Expressions reflecting dedication, hard work, and fairness were important parts of Johnson's public vocabulary. He was "working overtime," we must "do everything we can," he was engaged in "a continuous dialogue" with "responsible men of conviction and good will" to improve life "for every man, woman and child."

Johnson was convinced that world resources permitted the solution of all problems if only people of "good will" could meet privately and "reason together." Only misunderstandings, which could be worked out through private bargaining, stood in the way of total world prosperity and peace (Kearns, 1976, p. 194).

Verbal Analysis

Let us now look at Johnson's verbal scores. Figure 7-1 shows that, along with Eisenhower, he was the least impersonal of the Presidents. Johnson's nonpersonal references score was among the lowest of all post-World War II Presidents. He scored rather high in most "emotional" categories, as we might expect from the description of his personality.

What else is notable about Johnson's speaking style? His assertiveness can be seen in the very frequent use of the first person singular and plural (*I* and *we*) as subjects of clauses. These are "executive" pronouns; they act on verbs. This verbal habit accurately portrays Johnson for the leader he was—active, usually taking the initiative, rarely simply waiting for things to happen.

Johnson's moderate *qualifiers* and *retractors* scores suggests an unimpaired ability to make decisions, to stick to them, and to be able to reconsider without being paralyzed by indecision. His use of *negatives* is among the least frequent of all the Presidents under study. Johnson, the master of compromise and negotiation, was neither alienated from reality nor stubbornly oppositional.

How can we square these comments with Johnson's disastrous handling of the Vietnam war? Was not his inability to correctly interpret the movement of historical forces in Southeast Asia a reflection of an unwillingness to come to terms with an unpleasant reality? Not necessarily. We must recall that Johnson never considered himself an expert in foreign affairs; he relied heavily on his advisors, the "best and brightest" that had been brought to Washington by John F. Kennedy. Johnson's failure was less a matter of stubbornness and denial than of a certain mindset, a way of looking at the world that grew naturally out of his background and life's experiences. As Kearns points out, Johnson viewed foreigners as he did Americans, people desirous of material well-being who could be bought off by the proper rewards. He could not understand that religious and nationalist feelings might, at least for a time, be stronger motivating forces (Kearns, 1976).

Johnson's experiences in the 1930s and 1940s had also convinced him that appeasement of aggressors was a dangerous policy that might lead to a larger conflict. To him, appeasing North Vietnam was like giving in to Hitler. Defeat in Vietnam would lead to the feared "domino effect" and the loss of all Southeast Asia. If this constitutes denial, it was an affliction that struck a majority of both major parties as well as the leadership of the trade unions (Kearns, 1976, p. 95).

SUMMARY

Our survey of Lyndon B. Johnson's verbal style during his Presidential news conferences shows that a number of personality traits described by biographers and historians were revealed in his verbal behavior. Johnson's commanding manner was reflected in his attempt to control the timing, place, and agendas of the news conferences; in his curt responses to unwelcome questions; and in his interruptions of reporters when irritated. He did not tolerate criticism very well; Johnson would sometimes use news conferences to answer published attacks of his public or private behavior even when no questions were asked about these subjects.

Johnson's commanding personality was also revealed in his imperial verbal style. Third person references to "the President" and the frequent use of the "imperial" *we* are verbal testimony to his grandiosity.

Although extreme in temperament, Johnson was by no means an oppositional person. As a "consensus leader," he looked for the positive strivings in others in order to build coalitions.

Johnson's speech conveyed a great deal of emotion, although his scores in the "feelings" categories are somewhat below those of Eisenhower. His speech pattern reflects an ability to make decisions and a capacity to reconsider without becoming paralyzed or impulsive. These findings are consistent with descriptions of Johnson's behavior by those who knew him well.

CHAPTER 11

Richard M. Nixon

After an extremely controversial career, characterized by great political victories and equally significant defeats, Richard M. Nixon was elected to the Presidency when the Democratic Party split over the conduct of the Vietnam war. Promising to bring U.S. soldiers home in a "peace with honor," Nixon managed a close victory over Hubert Humphrey, who was chained to an unpopular and losing war effort in Southeast Asia.

Nixon brought to the Presidency a keen intelligence, which he applied with unexpected flexibility to foreign affairs. An admirer of French President Charles DeGaulle, Nixon, the conservative, anti-Communist Republican leader, was able to do for the United States what DeGaulle did for France—rescue his country from a self-destructive, narrow foreign policy defined by hawks of both political parties. Unfortunately, Nixon was unable to rescue himself from his own self-destructive political behavior, which resulted in his being the first U.S. President to resign from office.

PERSONALITY PROFILE

Richard M. Nixon has been described as a highly intelligent, analytical, and ambitious man. In many ways he is competitive, even combative. An admirer of well-bred, graceful people, Nixon can be socially awkward and physically clumsy. In the presence of individuals he greatly respects, his behavior appears deferential, almost obsequious. Nixon is very sensitive to slights and greatly appreciates praise and loyalty (Rather & Gates, 1974). Fearful of unstructured situations, Nixon is methodical and well prepared for his assignments. He is said to be an avid reader and a good listener.

Nixon has been described as a private, even a solitary man. He prefers the company of reserved, unemotional, and predictable individuals, although for brief periods he enjoys and can profit intellectually from the stimulation of flamboyant personalities (Rather & Gates, 1974). Generally able to pursue logical, carefully conceived plans, Nixon can behave under pressure in vacillating, contradictory, and even irrational ways. This is most apt to happen when he feels threatened by rivals or enemies.

To all except family and a few close associates, Nixon appears distant and aloof. Despite a combative temperament, he dislikes personal confrontations. It is difficult for him to be insulting or even severe with anyone in personal, one-on-one encounters. The attacks on political enemies, for which Nixon is famous, have always taken place in public settings. Although he does not cultivate kindliness as part of his public image, Nixon has been known to perform many quiet acts of generosity.

LEADERSHIP STYLE

Richard Nixon has been accused of continuing and expanding the "imperial Presidency." According to Schlesinger, he displayed "more monarchical yearnings than any of his predecessors. He plainly reveled in the ritual of the office" (1973, p. 218). More secretive even than Johnson, he centralized the powers of government in the White House. "He tried to shield himself . . . from direct question or challenge" (Schlesinger, 1973, p. 222).

Schlesinger believes that Nixon's style of leadership was genuinely revolutionary, that he was moving "towards rule by Presidential decree" (p. 246). "His model lay not in Britain but in France—in the France of Louis Napoleon and Charles DeGaulle" (p. 254).

Nixon's justification for this unusual concentration of power in the White House had to do with his view of the world as one "of unrelenting crisis, in which the United States, personified by its President, was assailed by a host of remorseless enemies" (p. 256).

Ironically, partly because of his own imaginative initiatives, the world during the Nixon Presidency was a lot safer than it had been before. By defusing the hostile confrontations with the Soviet Union and China, Nixon provided the nation with a period of "negotiation" rather than "confrontation" and Americans could breathe a bit easier. To Nixon, the "enemies" were more domestic than foreign—the "Eastern Establishment," the "liberals," and, most of all, the press.

Vindictive and unforgiving, Nixon came to believe that he was justified in using any means available to him to frustrate and defeat his
political enemies.

NIXON AND THE PRESS

It was inevitable that a leader as solitary, secretive, and sensitive as
Richard Nixon would have major problems with journalists. He
was impatient with the press, resentful about what he considered to
be unfair treatment in the past. During his unsuccessful campaign
for the Presidency in 1960, Nixon and his advisors assumed that
the press would be opposed to him no matter what he said or did
(White, 1961, pp. 329–330). Little or no attempt was made to cultivate journalists in the way Kennedy and Johnson did. Nixon believed that the safest course of action was to keep the press at a
distance, to treat reporters with a minimum of respect, and not to
expect their support. As President he *did* expect the media, as pa-
triotic Americans, to support his unpopular and difficult decisions
(Schlesinger, 1973).

Nixon's awkwardness, combativeness, and sensitivity made him
an easy target for political enemies. His frequent slips of the tongue
when under stress and his outbursts against reporters were well-
known to the public before Nixon's election to the Presidency. As
President, Nixon intended to present a more dignified and cool
appearance to the press. He would be polite, respectful, but distant.
He would limit his news conferences to infrequent, well-prepared
meetings. In that way, the excesses of the past, so damaging to his
career, could be avoided. As we shall see, Nixon largely succeeded
in his strategy during the first year of his Presidency. During his
second administration, as he became more and more embroiled in
domestic crises, Nixon regressed to old self-destructive habits and
once again lashed out against the press.

NIXON'S NEWS CONFERENCES

Determined not to expose himself to frequent public questioning,
Nixon held only eight news conferences during the first year in office. Only three of the eight news conferences had opening announcements. Nixon is the only post-World War II President to have
averaged more qualifiers per 1000 words in his opening remarks than

during the question and answer periods, although the difference is not significant (9.5 vs. 9.1). This suggests that his opening remarks were extemporaneous and that he carefully prepared for questions he assumed the journalists would ask. Nixon's responses were generally well-organized and concise.

The tone of Nixon's press conferences was very serious. There were few attempts at humor. During the "honeymoon" phase of Nixon's Presidency, he was polite and respectful, if somewhat distant, with the reporters, always addressing them as "Mr." or "Miss," never by their first names.

Nixon's grasp of the facts and issues was impressive. Somewhat pedantic in his manner, he was, nevertheless, a good teacher, particularly when explaining the tactics of foreign leaders. The following excerpt is an example of Nixon, the teacher, in action. The President had just been asked a question about the tense situation in West Berlin. Nixon gave the following reasons why he felt the Soviets would not provoke a crisis at that time:

THE PRESIDENT: At this moment, based on the conversations that I have had myself with various European leaders and also the conversation that I and others have had with the representatives of the Soviet Union, I believe that the Soviet Union does not want to have the situation in West Berlin heated up to the point that it would jeopardize some—what they consider to be—more important negotiations at the highest level with the United States. And because these negotiations, in effect, are in the wings, I think I could predict that the Soviet Union will use its influence to cool off the West Berlin situation, rather than to heat it up (Public Papers of the Presidents of the United States, 1971, p. 182).

It is well known that Nixon, under certain kinds of stress, would make slips of the tongue. Even during the first year "honeymoon" period with the press, when he was well in control of himself, Nixon made an occasional revealing slip, as in the news conference of June 19, 1969. Responding to a question about Nelson Rockefeller's Latin American tour, Nixon stated: "In my conversations with [Columbian] President Lleras, the talking paper that President—Governor Rockefeller—a Freudian slip—the talking paper that Governor Rockefeller gave me was extremely helpful" (Public Papers of the Presidents of the United

States, 1971, p. 479). The reader will note that Nixon immediately recognized, corrected, and analyzed his slip, suggesting a good level of ego functioning. When under greater stress, as during the news conferences held in the Watergate period, Nixon's slips were extremely revealing and went by unnoticed and uncorrected by the President. Consider the following interchange between reporter Bob Haiman of the St. Petersburg *Times* and President Nixon at the Annual Convention of the Associated Press Managing Editors Association, Orlando, Florida, on November 17, 1973 (Public Papers of the Presidents of the United States, 1975, p. 952).

MR. HAIMAN: When Mr. Ehrlichman and Mr. Haldeman left your Administration, you said they were guiltless in the Watergate affair, and they were, quote, two of the finest public servants you had ever known, end quote. After what has transpired and been revealed since then, do you still feel the same way about both men and both statements?

THE PRESIDENT: First, I hold that both men and others who have been charged are guilty until I have evidence that they are not guilty, and I know that every newspaperman and newspaperwoman in this whole audience would agree with that statement.

Nixon did not notice his slip, which, of course, was an accurate assessment of the guilt of his associates. Later in the news conference, a journalist brought Nixon's slip to his attention and he corrected it.

During Nixon's first year in office, he was able to control his combativeness. Under the stress of the Watergate scandal, he began to regress to his old press-baiting habits. The following excerpt from the former President's final formal news conference on October 26, 1973, illustrates the bad feeling between Nixon and the White House press corps (Public Papers of the Presidents of the United States, 1975, p. 905):

REPORTER: Mr. President, you have lambasted the television networks pretty well. Could I ask you, at the risk of reopening an obvious wound, you say after you have put on a lot of heat that you don't blame anyone. I find that a little puzzling. What is it about the television coverage of you in these past weeks and months that has so aroused your anger?

THE PRESIDENT: Don't get the impression that you arouse my anger. [Laughter]

REPORTER: I'm afraid, sir, that I have that impression. [Laughter]

THE PRESIDENT: You see, one can only be angry with those he respects.

Favorite Words and Phrases

Nixon's speaking style can be rather easily identified by certain words and phrases. Some of his favorites were "incidentally," "shall we say," "move forward," "frankly," "as you know," and "go down that road." Perhaps the most famous Nixonian phrase, frequently used by the former President's many impersonators, was his desire to "make things clear" or to make things "perfectly clear." Some version of this phrase appeared at least once during each news conference.

Verbal Analysis

Charges that Nixon continued strongly in the direction of establishing an "imperial Presidency" are confirmed in the frequent use of the "imperial" *we* and in his referring to "the President" in the third person. During his very first Presidential press conference, on January 27, 1969, Nixon stated:

> Now there is a second immediate point that I have noted. That is the fact that there will be another meeting in Warsaw. *We* look forward to that meeting. *We* will be interested to see what the Chinese Communist representatives may have to say at that meeting. . . . (Public Papers of the Presidents of the United States, 1971, p. 16).

Later in the same news conference, Nixon noted that "We have one President at a time, and . . . he must continue to be President until he leaves office on January 20" (Public Papers of the Presidents of the United States, 1971, p. 21).

Like most well-prepared verbal responses, Nixon's answers to reporters' questions were not reflected by extreme verbal scores. His use of personal pronouns ($I + we$) was modest, the I/we ratio tilted in the direction of I. Nixon was proud of being President, often referring to himself as "the President" or as "Commander-in-Chief." Although formal and polite with the reporters—at least during the first year—his controlled combativeness did reveal itself somewhat in his fairly frequent use of *direct references*. Nixon could not keep himself from getting involved with the journalists when challenged, although he did not allow the 1969 press conferences to become arenas for mutual recriminations as they did during the Watergate scandal.

Nixon's distrust of his ability to control himself with the press is perhaps best revealed by the infrequent number of news conferences he held. Only Ronald Reagan—for quite different reasons—held fewer press conferences than Nixon during the first year in office.

In keeping with the reserve and formality of his press conferences, Nixon's *nonpersonal references* score was rather high. His use of those categories we have identified as "emotional" was modest. Under conditions that he could carefully control—infrequent and well-prepared news conferences—Nixon's use of *qualifiers* and *retractors* was moderate, indicating an ability to make decisions and to stick to them.

Fearful of unstructured situations, Nixon tended to avoid encounters that would bring out the dark, combative side of his personality. Readers of my book, *Verbal Behavior*, know that Nixon's verbal style in the unprepared and unrehearsed Watergate conversations was quite different from what it was during his news conferences. A comparison of the two styles tells us something of Nixon's response to stress (1981, pp. 111–136).

During the Watergate conversations, Nixon's *I/we ratio, negatives, retractions, expressions of feeling,* and *evaluators* scores were much higher and his *nonpersonal references* score much lower than during the 1969 Presidential news conferences. Together these findings suggest a self-preoccupied leader stubbornly fighting to maintain his situation, sometimes unable to assess the reality of the dangers he faced, and, perhaps most important of all, subject to impulsive behavior.

WHY NIXON FASCINATES US

Few people can be objective about Richard Nixon. Most ex-Presidents cease to be of public interest after leaving office. Nixon continues to stimulate strong feelings of affection and hatred 10 years after his resignation from office. Why? Some of Nixon's fascination undoubtedly has to do with the apparently contradictory nature of his personality and policies. An avowed anti-Communist who built his career on red-baiting his political opponents, Nixon opened the door to the People's Republic of China and established practical and cordial relations with the Soviet Union. His most vociferous enemies on the left agree that Nixon's accomplishments in foreign policy were substantial and long-lasting. Like DeGaulle, his hero and model, the conservative Nixon was able to rescue the United States from a foreign policy impasse without appearing to be "soft on Communism."

Nixon's apparent contradictions were not limited to foreign policy. Some of his domestic initiatives, such as welfare reform and the restructuring of the nation's cities, were truly revolutionary and unexpected, in view of his right-wing reputation.

I do not believe that the contradictory quality of Nixon's career is solely responsible for his hold on the imagination of the American people. There is a certain pragmatic, amoral streak in Nixon's character that appeals to most of us, friend or foe. It is difficult to watch Nixon on television without some mixture of amusement and indignation. At his Machiavellian best, Nixon does and says what others think but dare not do. He is like a child or pet animal who allows us to enjoy the vicarious pleasures of uninhibited egoism. How is this quality revealed in Nixon's speech? We see it most clearly in his explanations of his behavior in stressful situations. In defending his actions during the Watergate affair, for example, Nixon carefully reviewed in public the various choices he had in dealing with the crisis. During the news conference of August 22, 1973, he was asked about the raising of funds for the Watergate defendants. In this portion of his reply, the reader will note the moral weakness of Nixon's position as he recalls a conversation with John Dean (Public Papers of the Presidents of the United States, 1975, p. 721):

PRESIDENT: Mr. Dean said also on March 21 that there was an attempt, as he put it, to blackmail the White House defendants. Incidentally, that defendant has denied it, but at least this was what Mr. Dean had claimed, and that unless certain amounts of money were paid—I think it was $120,000 for attorneys' fees and other support—that this particular defendant would make a statement, not with regard to Watergate, but with regard to some national security matters in which Mr. Ehrlichman had particular responsibility. My reaction, very briefly, was this: I said, 'As you look at this,' I said, 'isn't it quite obvious, first, that if it is going to have any chance to succeed, that these individuals aren't going to sit there in jail for 4 years? They are going to have clemency; isn't that correct?' He said, 'Yes.' I said, 'We can't give clemency.' He agreed. Then, I went to another point. I said, 'The second point is that isn't it also quite obvious, as far as this is concerned, that while we could raise the money'—and he indicated in answer to my question, it would probably take a million dollars over 4 years to take care of this defendant, and others, on this kind of basis—the problem was, how do you get the money to them, and also, how do you get around the problem of clemency, because they are not going to stay in jail simply because their families are being taken care of. And so, that was why I concluded, as Mr. Haldeman recalls perhaps and did testify very effectively, one, when I said, 'John, it is wrong, it won't work. We can't give clemency, and we have got to get this story out.'

In comparing Nixon's Watergate comments with his remarks about the Soviet Union's international behavior on pages 77–78, the reader will note the same objective, pragmatic analysis of possibilities and motivations. In paying only lip service to the moral aspects of the Watergate affair, Nixon showed that he could not distinguish between personal and national interest. He understood the importance of integrity, but it was only one factor among many others to be taken into account when making a decision.

SUMMARY

One of the best prepared of all the post-World War II Presidents for his infrequent news conferences, Richard Nixon was able, during noncrisis periods, to keep his relations with the press on a polite, reserved basis. During the first year in office, he was impressive in his grasp of the issues and in his ability to explain policy—particularly foreign policy—to the American people. Nixon's use of "emotional" verbal categories was modest, in line with his polite reserve. He eshewed opening remarks, preferring the give and take of the question and answer periods, for which he was extremely well prepared.

Nixon's use of *qualifiers* and *retractors* shows an unimpaired ability to make decisions and to stick to them when not under stress. Combative when attacked, Nixon has been extraordinarily sensitive to criticism and very fearful of uncontrolled situations. Several times during his career he cracked under pressure and publicly demonstrated loss of control. Under stress, Nixon shows remarkable changes in his verbal style. His use of *negatives, expressions of feeling, retractors,* and *evaluators* increases; his use of *nonpersonal references* decreases. This suggests a tendency toward impulsive behavior, a decrease in the ability to interpret reality, and an increase in oppositional behavior. There is also evidence that Nixon under pressure may become clinically depressed; his scores during the Watergate conversations cannot be distinguished from those of clinically depressed psychiatric inpatients (Weintraub, 1981, pp. 111–136).

In conclusion, Nixon's behavior during his news conferences as well as their infrequency indicates a leader who functions best when he can avoid excessive stimulation and can prepare carefully for public performances. Nixon avoided the press during his two campaigns for the Presidency, perhaps realizing the danger of losing control when besieged by "enemy" reporters. As President he gradually withdrew from frequent contacts with the public, allowing the Presidency to be protected by "gatekeepers" like A.R. Haldeman. The price he paid for his withdrawal was to hear only what his staff thought would please him. Greater accessibility to the press and their criticism might have allowed Nixon to avoid the events that prematurely terminated his Presidency.

CHAPTER 12

Gerald R. Ford

Appointed and confirmed as the 40th Vice President of the United States, following the resignation of Spiro Agnew, Gerald Ford became President of the United States when the Watergate scandal forced Richard Nixon from office. Ford was the only President never to win a national election. In his many years in the House of Representatives, he never had been seriously considered as a Presidential possibility. But if Watergate gave him an opportunity to lead the nation, his decision to pardon Richard Nixon may have contributed to his failure to win the Presidency on his own.

PERSONALITY PROFILE

Although observers of Gerald Ford differ about certain aspects of his personality and style, there is general agreement that, unlike his two predecessors, Johnson and Nixon, he is a simple and straightforward man. Like Eisenhower, Ford is capable of lying for his country, but deceptive behavior is not one of his characteristics. Estimates of Ford's intelligence vary. His academic accomplishments suggest that he has a good, if uncomplicated, mind. Richard Reeves has described Ford as "solid, inertial, naive," with no instinct for power and manipulation (1976, p. 26). He is extremely steady and predictable in most situations.

Most Ford watchers agree that he is a "good" man although partisan and conservative (Reeves, 1976). Unlike Johnson and Nixon, Ford is open and honest and did not try to cover up Presidential mistakes. Relaxed and direct, he did not develop a "personality cult" as did his three predecessors. Simple and humble, Ford almost never used the "imperial" *we* during press conferences nor did he refer to himself as "the President."

If Johnson and Nixon were hypersensitive to criticism, Ford has been almost immune to personal attack. He has been quoted as saying, "It just doesn't do any good to get mad. It never solves anything. You just have to move on" (Casserly, 1977, p. 37). To Ford, criticism is a fact of life that a politician has to live with.

Ford has been described as exceptionally steady and calm, not given to mood swings or sharp emotional reactions. Like Lyndon Johnson, another legislative leader, Ford looked for consensus rather than confrontation. Unlike Johnson, he did not seek to dominate those around him. He was more apt to accommodate himself to circumstances rather than bend them to his will.

As the minority leader in the House during decades of Democratic administrations, Ford learned to tolerate and survive adversity. He was able to maintain a hopeful and optimistic attitude when other men would have been frustrated by long years of defeat.

LEADERSHIP STYLE

If Ford's open, honest, and candid personality drew much praise from critics, his leadership style as President was subject to negative criticism. As a Congressional leader by consensus, he was very much a team player. Yet he has been described as unprepared to be President (Reeves, 1976). A better listener than a reader, Ford disliked long memoranda. He preferred "yes or no" options without "a lot of complications" (Reeves, 1976, p. 32). Ford has been described as "a realist," "a man who called the shots objectively without major ideological or philosophical hangups" (Casserly, 1977, p. 21).

Ford was seen by many as lacking goals and strategy, simply trying to solve immediate problems "on a hit and run basis" (Casserly, 1977, p. 39). He apparently never forcefully established the fact that he was President. After being accused of passivity, he would, from time to time, take matters into his own hands and act boldly, even impulsively, as in the dramatic shakeup of his staff on November 2, 1975 (Reeves, 1976). The events of November 2nd, however, were not typical of the way Ford treated his appointees. In general, he was extremely loyal to them. He has been described as a leader who was more interested in survival than leadership, in accommodation than compromise, in harmony than confrontation. He was accused of not being able to distinguish between "compromising moral principles and compromising legislative positions" (Casserly, 1977, p. 237).

At his worst, Ford was described as a "waffler" (Casserly, 1977, p. 288). Perhaps the most damning criticism of Ford was the following: "The leadership, the inspiration, the intellectual integrity, the courage of conviction, the trust and belief of men—all of these qualities necessary for the highest office in our land appear wanting in Gerald Ford" (Casserly, 1977, p. 291).

FORD AND THE PRESS

Reporters liked Ford and wanted him to succeed after Nixon's disgrace. Like most Americans, they didn't want a second failed Presidency (Reeves, 1976). Unlike Nixon, Ford genuinely liked reporters and his press relations were good (Casserly, 1977). As President, he made no attempt to be secretive with the press.

During news conferences, Ford was polite and respectful with the journalists. He generally addressed them as Mr. or Miss. When asked a difficult question, he did not become defensive or irritable. Ford would go out of his way to congratulate a reporter who had been honored for his work, usually in a good-humored, teasing manner. The following exchange, during the May 6, 1975, news conference, was typical of his way of courting the press (Public Papers of the Presidents of the United States, 1977, p. 644). Reporter Mary McGrory of the Washington Star-News had raised her hand to ask a question:

PRESIDENT: Miss McGrory, may I congratulate you on your Pulitzer Prize, and I am delighted to recognize you.

Although Ford occasionally teased reporters, his remarks were more affectionate than hostile. There was none of the combativeness so characteristic of Nixon. The following exchange with Helen Thomas of United Press International is typical of Ford's good-natured bantering with the journalists:

MISS THOMAS: Mr. President, when you were a Congressman and called for the impeachment of Justice Douglas, did you have access or were you slipped any secret FBI data?
PRESIDENT: I do not know what the source was of information that was given to me, but I was given information by a

high-ranking official of the Department of Justice. I do not know what the source of that information was.

MISS THOMAS: Was it Attorney General Mitchell, then Attorney General Mitchell?

PRESIDENT: It was not the Attorney General, John Mitchell.

MISS THOMAS: Was it FBI Director J. Edgar Hoover?

PRESIDENT: It was not. Two times and you are out, Helen. [Laughter] (Public Papers of the Presidents of the United States, 1977, pp. 184–185).

GERALD FORD'S NEWS CONFERENCES

During his first year in office, Ford held 19 news conferences. He made opening remarks in 11 of them. The tone of his remarks was generally serious. Ford's speaking style was clear and simple. The average length of his responses to questions was moderate; there were few of the lengthy answers characteristic of Kennedy and Johnson. Ford did not try to evade questions he couldn't or did not wish to answer. When faced with such a question, he simply stated that he could not answer it and usually gave his reasons. Ford was obviously comfortable with the journalists, treating them politely, accepting criticism graciously, and rarely responding defensively to pointed questions.

Favorite Words and Expressions

What distinguishes Ford's speech is the very large number of *qualifiers* and *evaluators*. He rarely spoke in a categorical way, generally qualifying his statements with expressions like "in my judgment," "it seems to me," "I can assure you that," and so on. Ford's *evaluators* reflected concern over what was good, right, fair, realistic, honest, balanced, and rational.

Ford's Openness with the Press

More than most Presidents, Ford was able to share his inner thoughts and feelings with the press, as in the following exchange during the May 6, 1975, news conference (Public Papers of the Presidents of the United States, 1977, pp. 650–651):

REPORTER: May I ask you something, sir, and simply a matter of style and nothing of substance. Reading Mr. Hersey, who has spent a week with you, and reading others, you seem to be a kind of peaceful, quiet man, a placid man. Do you ever get mad at people? Do you ever chew people out? Do you yell? Do you fire people? Do you kick people around?

PRESIDENT: I have learned to control my temper. I get very upset internally, but I have learned that that is not the best way to solve a problem. I do have occasional outbursts on the golf course, but in dealing with people I have found that the best way to meet a personnel problem or to handle a serious matter where a decision has to be made—that if you can keep cool, you can make a better decision. I have learned that over a long period of time.

As I have indicated above, Ford would take every opportunity to praise a reporter who had been honored in any way. He often praised members of his administration and fellow Republicans. His answers to questions were full of phrases like "fine public servant," "good governor," "excellent administrator," and so on.

Verbal Analysis

Ford's opening remarks were generally brief but well-prepared. His use of *qualifiers* was about 1.5 per 1000 words, suggesting very careful preparation.

Ford's verbal pattern during the question and answer periods was an extremely interesting one. Of the seven post-World War II Presidents, he scored highest in *qualifiers* and *evaluators*, lowest in *negatives* and *retractors*. Ford's scores closely parallel the biographical comments I have summarized above. A score of 16 *qualifiers* per 1000 words is quite high for a press conference and indicates indecisiveness.

Ford was moderate or low in his use of "emotional" categories, such as *expressions of feeling, adverbial intensifiers, personal references,* and *direct references*. This undoubtedly contributed to the blandness of his verbal style.

Although Ford emerges as an extremely cautious, even indecisive leader, his low *retractors* score suggests that once he makes a decision he sticks to it. A rather low *negatives* score indicates that Ford is positive and not oppositional in his approach to problems and people. A low *negatives* score also indicates an ability to face reality, a disinclination to seek comfort in denial.

The following excerpt from the February 4, 1975, press

conference demonstrates Ford's frequent use of *qualifiers*. Note how it imparts a "wishy-washy" quality to his verbal style (Public Papers of the Presidents of the United States, 1977, p. 185).

REPORTER: Do you think the economic situation, though, that you will be able to lick it, of course, increasing your chances [of being elected President]?

PRESIDENT: *I believe* that the economic situation in 1976 will be an improving economic picture. It won't *perhaps* be as good as we would like it, but *I believe* that unemployment will be going down and employment will be going up, and we will be doing a considerable amount better in the battle against inflation than we did in the last 12 months. So, with the optimism that *I think* will come from more employment, less unemployment, and a battle against inflation, *I think* the economic circumstances will be good enough to justify at least my seeking reelection.

Of the post-World War II Presidents, Ford had the lowest density of *adverbial intensifiers*, suggesting that he was the least histrionic of the group. All in all, Ford emerges as a straightforward and direct, if bland and colorless leader.

As already noted above, Ford had the highest *evaluators* score of all the Presidents and by a considerable margin. This is certainly an accurate verbal reflection of his concern with what was appropriate, right, and useful. The high *evaluators* score also mirrors Ford's optimism and frequent praise of aides and fellow Republicans.

Ford's Response to Stress

Ford's biographers have described him as an unusually steady President, one who rarely lost his composure. And yet he would occasionally act impulsively under stress. How is this trait revealed in Ford's verbal behavior?

In order to see how Ford handled stress, I scored his answers to a number of pointed questions. The results suggested several trends. There was a substantial decrease in *nonpersonal references* and an increase in *direct references*, suggesting more personal involvement when under fire. There was also an increase in the use of *retractors*, indicating the possibility of impulsive action. An increase in the *we* and *me* categories suggested a waffling response to stress, endless consultation with aides, and a passive stance.

SUMMARY

Let us summarize Ford's verbal findings. His high *qualifiers* score suggests a cautious, indecisive leader who could stick to decisions once he made them (moderate *retractors* score). Ford's low *negatives* score indicates a positive approach to problems. He was not oppositional or defensive. Cool and slow to be aroused, he was one of the more reserved of the post-World War II Presidents (low in most of the "emotional" categories). Ford was direct and candid during his news conferences.

Under stress, Ford showed an exaggeration of his passivity (higher *me* score) and a tendency to waffle (continued high *qualifiers* score and an increased use of *retractors*). Rarely, Ford acted impulsively under pressure, a course of action wafflers sometimes follow when stressed over a long period of time.

CHAPTER 13

Jimmy Carter

The first politician from the Deep South to be elected President since the Civil War, Jimmy Carter brought to the White House a number of contrasting personality characteristics. Let us briefly consider them.

PERSONALITY PROFILE

Carter has been described as highly intelligent, disciplined, and hardworking. An early riser, he avoids alcohol and is extremely careful with money. Carter is said to have an almost photographic memory (Mazlish & Diamond, 1979).

Carter's self-discipline includes a tight rein on his emotions. He is quoted as saying, "I doubt that anyone has ever seen me livid. . . . I really cannot recall a time when I lost control of myself or even lost control of my temper" (Mazlish & Diamond, 1979, p. 16). His anger is more apt to be expressed in sarcasm than in fits of temper.

Biographers have been puzzled by what appear to be polar opposites in Carter's personality. He is generally considered to be shy, yet self-confident; gentle, yet "steely." Carter has been accused of rigidity, of being unable to reverse himself once he has made a decision. It is difficult for him to admit that he has made a mistake. He can be quick and impatient (Mazlish & Diamond, 1979). Carter remains a puzzle at the same time that he is the most self-revealing of the post-World War II Presidents. There seems to be no question about his personal life that he is unwilling to answer.

Carter has been described as steady and consistent, adhering to fixed, long-term goals but extremely flexible and realistic about the short-term measures that may be needed to achieve them. He has been called a complex President. Carter sacrificed the short-term political advantages of simplicity to the long-term advantages of presenting complicated issues to the U.S. people, a practice that made him seem indecisive (Mazlish & Diamond, 1979, p. 264).

LEADERSHIP STYLE

Carter's view of the Presidency was that government must reflect the innate goodness of the people and that the President must go directly to the people, over the heads of the Congress and the political parties, if necessary. Yet he did not see himself as a "heroic" President. Like Ford, he did not wish to be an "imperial" President; he often emphasized the limits of the President's authority. He had no need to prove himself in the Presidency by seeking out and winning conflicts (Mazlish & Diamond, 1979).

Like Lyndon Johnson, Carter was a master of detail. Although he insisted on making all important decisions, he was able to delegate tasks without interfering in the work of his subordinates.

Carter has been called a good and decent man. He tries to tell the truth, has supported human rights around the world, and, in general, has taken a high moral position on most issues. On the other hand, he has stubbornly defended friends and relatives whose behavior has not been above reproach (Miller, 1978).

Carter made political hay by presenting himself as an outsider to Washington politics. However helpful this stance was in winning the Presidency, it proved to be a liability in governing the nation. "Cool and aloof," he resented making deals to get things done (Miller, 1978, pp. 29–30). Yet he was not successful in appealing directly to the U.S. people for support of his programs. Lacking the charisma of a Roosevelt or a Reagan, Carter could not mobilize public opinion to help him in his struggles with Congress. In the end, he was forced to seek the help of Democratic Party leaders, demonstrating that he could adapt himself to political realities.

Carter had little appetite for conflict within his administration. Major decisions were made only by him. There was to be "only one star in his administration" (Miller, 1978, p. 88). Unlike Eisenhower and Ford, Carter wanted detailed recommendations sent to him for decisions. He resisted brief, simplified summaries. Although elected as a "technical" person, Carter's administration has been accused of lacking managerial competence on all levels (Mazlish & Diamond, 1979).

I have already suggested that Carter consciously chose to deemphasize the imperial quality of the Presidency. He was determined to bring the office back to the people. His studied informality, his walking down Pennsylvania Avenue on Inauguration Day, his dressing in a sweater and jeans—all these symbolic acts of "pompicide" nevertheless had "a high component of the personal" (Miller, 1978, p. 88).

Carter has been described as a person who needs power only to accomplish worthy goals, not to bolster an insecure self. Yet there is the highly competitive side of his personality. He likes to run (literally as well as figuratively) and he likes to win. This competitive side of Carter has sometimes caused him to become cruel, particularly during tough electoral campaigns. In the last stages of his first Presidential campaign, he broke a promise not to attack his opponent in personal ways. Carter questioned President Ford's character and intelligence. His strident attacks nearly cost him the election.

Carter has sometimes been described as more of a manager than a leader, a politician who, with the best of motives, tries to discern the wishes of the people and then serve them in the way they want (Mazlish & Diamond, 1979). As candidate and President, he did not offer a vision of the future but claimed that he could lead the United States into the electronic age better than his rivals (Miller, 1978).

CARTER'S RELATIONSHIP WITH THE PRESS

In some ways, Carter seemed tailor-made to be idolized by the press. Of rural background, an outsider, and amazingly candid about himself and his family, he gave the reporters a number of sensational stories. In addition, Carter's views and aspirations as a liberal Democrat were in line with the views of many journalists. Yet he was not liked by the reporters. Part of the problem was Carter's standoffishness, stubbornness, and self-righteousness. There is also a vindictive side to him. Carter is sensitive to personal criticism and showed his sensitivity during the news conferences. Unlike Eisenhower, Kennedy, and Reagan, he did not try to court the press. Shy and aloof, he could not relax easily with them. His sarcastic humor was sometimes directed against the reporters.

Well-informed and on top of the issues, Carter tried to outsmart the journalists, demonstrate his superior command of the facts. This combination of aloofness, sensitivity, and competitiveness did not endear him to the White House press corps.

Carter's wish to be open and honest about his personal life sometimes backfired and caused him political harm. His famous *Playboy* interview, for example, in which he tried to be frank about his sexual fantasies, lost him support among his more conservative backers. His decision to devote an entire press conference to the activities of brother Billy was a political blunder. Under similar circumstances, Franklin Roosevelt and Ronald Reagan joked their way out of embarrassing disclosures and refused to allow their private lives to become the subjects of public interviews.

CARTER'S PRESIDENTIAL NEWS CONFERENCES

During the first year of his administration, Jimmy Carter held 22 news conferences. His responses to reporters' questions were rather long, sometimes over 400 words.

Carter began 17 of the 22 press conferences with introductory remarks. His use of *qualifiers* during the opening remarks averaged more than 10 per 1000 words, indicating that he was probably speaking extemporaneously. Priding himself on his command of the facts, Carter is said not to have needed extensive briefing before news conferences (Miller, 1978).

Carter's manner with the reporters was somewhat formal and indirect. He avoided addressing members of the press by name, often calling upon them by pointing or nodding. When he did address a journalist directly, he almost always used the formal "Mr." when speaking to male reporters. Carter addressed women journalists somewhat less formally, using their first names or "Miss" with about equal frequency. He is the only post-World War II President to address male and female reporters differently.

The tone of Carter's press conferences was solemn. His occasional attempts at humor were labored and sardonic and, at times, at the expense of the reporters. Consider, for example, the following excerpt from the February 8, 1977, news conference:

PRESIDENT: I was concerned, for instance, when the AP reporter was expelled from Moscow. I had at first thought to retaliate by expelling the AP reporter from Washington. But I found out that was not the right approach to take (Public Papers of the Presidents of the United States, 1977, p. 100).

Carter's style of answering reporters' questions was to demonstrate a superior knowledge of the issues. As a result, his news conferences often became tedious recitals of facts. The following excerpt from the April 22, 1977, news conference demonstrates Carter's soporific response to a question about the Middle East:

PRESIDENT: I've continued my own study of the Middle Eastern question. As you know, I have met now with the Prime Minister of Israel and also with President Sadat of Egypt. Today I'll be meeting with Deputy Prime Minister and Foreign Minister Khadam of Syria. And early next month I'll meet with President Assad from Syria on a brief trip to Geneva. King Hussein will be here Sunday and Monday to meet with me (Public Papers of the Presidents of the United States, 1977, p. 702).

Carter's Sensitivity to Criticism

Carter presented himself to the public as a humble and modest leader, ready to admit his shortcomings and eager to learn. When his ability to perform in a particular situation was questioned, however, he was hurt and he showed it. The following exchange from the March 9, 1977, news conference illustrates Carter's sensitivity to implied criticism of his negotiating abilities:

REPORTER: What effect in your mind, if any, is the extent of debate in the Senate over Mr. Warnke's qualifications to be the chief SALT negotiator going to have eventually on our negotiating position?

PRESIDENT: I don't believe that the exact vote in the Senate on Mr. Warnke's confirmation will have a major effect on future negotiations with the Soviet Union on SALT. The obvious impression that concerns me is a demonstration of lack of confidence of the Senate in my own ability and attitudes as a chief negotiator. Obviously, as President, any decisions made with the Russians on reduction of atomic weapons would have to be approved by me (Public Papers of the Presidents of the United States, 1977, p. 345).

Carter had a competitive relationship with the press. At times, when annoyed, he would interrupt reporters, as in the following exchange during the April 15, 1977, news conference (p. 636).

REPORTER: Mr. President, the House, as you know, just recently passed the Harkin Amendment to the International Lending Institutions Act of 1977—

PRESIDENT: Yes, I know.

REPORTER: —which stipulates that the United States representative must vote "no" to countries who violate . . . human rights.

Here, Carter seemed to be irritated by the reporter's not assuming that he knew about the passage of the Harkin Amendment. He interrupted in a defensive way.

Favorite Words and Phrases

Some of Carter's favorite words were "obviously," "substantial," and "concerned." His answers to questions generally had a tone of extreme seriousness and high purpose. The sale of bombs to a foreign country "concerns me very much" (Public Papers of the Presidents of the United States, 1977, p. 93). He wished, without proceeding "too hastily, in a very careful and methodical way to demonstrate to the world that we are sincere" in disarmament talks (p. 96). He was "consistently and completely dedicated to the enhancement of human rights" (p. 100).

During his campaign for the Presidency, Carter discovered that voters responded favorably to his assertions that he didn't know all the answers. He continued this modest approach during his news conferences, answering criticism by stating that he had a lot to learn but was doing "the best I can." The theme of working in a sincere and honest manner to solve the nation's problems runs through all of Carter's press conferences. When such statements were insufficient to calm his questioners, he could become prickly and answer in a defensive or sarcastic way.

Verbal Analysis

Carter scored high in the *I, expressions of feeling,* and *adverbial intensifiers* categories and rather low in the use of *we, nonpersonal references,* and *explainers.* Taken together, these findings identify

Carter as one of the more expressive Presidents. His use of *direct references* was the lowest of all the Presidents, suggesting that Carter avoided direct interaction with the reporters, a reflection, perhaps, of his shyness.

Carter's use of *qualifying phrases* and *retractors* was somewhat above the mean, indicating a tendency to waffle. It has been reported that Carter became clinically depressed in 1966, after losing the Georgia gubernatorial primary (Mazlish & Diamond, 1979). Is there any evidence of depressive potential in his speaking style? Yes. Carter's scores in a number of categories associated with clinical depression—*I, expressions of feeling, personal references, evaluators,* and *adverbial intensifiers*—are above the mean for the seven post-World War II Presidents.

We have alluded earlier to Carter's alleged rigidity. Is there evidence of this trait in his speaking style? Yes. The reader will note that his *explainers* score is the lowest of all the Presidents. Carter spoke to the reporters in a categorical rather than in an explanatory manner. This conveyed an impression of preaching rather than reasoning, of arguing with facts rather than with reasons.

Carter's use of pronouns suggests that he was better able to share feelings than power. An outsider who won his party's nomination through direct appeals to the voters, Carter likely saw his Presidency as a "Jimmy Carter" Administration rather than one directed by the leader of a political party. He used *I* repeatedly when referring to problems to be analyzed, decisions to be made, credit to be assigned, and blame to be apportioned.

Carter's moderate *negatives* score indicates a generally positive approach to people and problems. He does not come across as highly oppositional, nor does he appear to be unable to consider both favorable and disagreeable sides of reality. Denial and negation do not appear to be strong personality traits.

Carter's *qualifiers* and *retractors* scores are only moderately high, suggesting that he could make and stick to decisions, yet reconsider when necessary. Under stress he could become indecisive, as his behavior during the Iranian crisis demonstrated.

SUMMARY

Jimmy Carter's grammatical choices are those of a "loner" in politics. He developed his own following, seized the machinery of government, and never really learned to share power. Sensitive and competitive, Carter was wounded by criticism and was unable to deal with reporters who attacked him. Carter's penchant for detail and his need to "do it himself" helped create the image of a leader who was, at times, in over his head. He did not succeed in conveying to the American people an impression of being in command, of being able to rise above the concrete details of government. Shy and reserved, Carter nevertheless revealed a great deal of himself, probably more than the public needed or wanted to know. Carter's use of "emotional" categories confirms this expressive side of him. His public behavior can best be described as "personal" but not engaging. A certain interpersonal sensitivity, which he could never overcome, worked against his political fortunes.

CHAPTER 14

Ronald Reagan

A former Democrat, movie actor, and Governor of California, Ronald Reagan was elected President as a Republican in 1980. Reagan's election was greatly facilitated by Jimmy Carter's inability to handle the Iranian hostage crisis, a failure that reinforced the American people's impression of him as a weak and ineffective leader.

PERSONALITY PROFILE

Because of Reagan's consummate skill as a politician-actor, it is not easy to separate out his personality traits from his public performances. He has been described as genial, amiable, courageous, a leader with stamina and "underlying toughness" (Drew, 1981, p. 121). Enormously self-confident, he is friendly and gregarious. Yet, he has been described by Elizabeth Drew as "always on stage. His remoteness from people, except for his wife and a few close friends, is striking." According to Drew, Reagan doesn't reach out, is not curious about people. "It's not just that he's on guard but that he is remote. His eyes don't engage, he doesn't engage" (Drew, 1981, p. 271).

Emotionally controlled in public, Reagan has a quick temper and can be irritable in private when things are not going his way. A "genuinely courteous and gracious man," Reagan has a stubborn streak that seems to have accentuated with age (Drew, 1985, p. 573). Proud and competitive, he has qualities of shrewdness, optimism, and conviction.

REAGAN THE COMMUNICATOR

Ronald Reagan has few equals in the ability to project himself as an effective leader. His "powers of communication under . . . the most important circumstances rank with the best in the history of American politics" (Drew, 1985, p. 712). Richard Reeves has called him "a hell of a salesman" (Reeves, 1976, p. 14). It is important to note that Reagan's effectiveness as a communicator lies primarily in his remarkable ability to deliver a prepared speech. Reeves has written: "With practiced moves and inflections, he has choked me up, swelled my proud American chest, made me laugh, then almost cry, and done magic with the hair on the back of my neck—and I don't particularly like him or a lot of what he has to say" (Reeves, 1976, p. 20). Much of Reagan's success as a speaker has to do with his ability to establish "an intimacy with the audience" (Drew, 1985, p. 524).

LEADERSHIP STYLE

Unlike Carter and Ford, Reagan has been able to convince the U.S. people that he is a strong, effective leader. Tall and masculine, he "looks the way we want a President to look. . . . [He] offers to the public a disposition that is amiable but capable of turning tough should the need arise (Drew, 1985, p. 712). He "sees simple truths and delivers a simple message" (p. 719).

Although he seeks his friends among the rich, Reagan's chief support has come from the middle-class and blue collar workers. He speaks the language of the common people.

At least during his first years in office, Reagan and his aides succeeded in hiding his Administration's internal squabbles from the American people. As a result, he appeared strong, consistent, unwavering. Reagan has been able to implement a strongly conservative economic program without seeming to be harsh or uncaring. He has successfully projected an image of a "regular guy" and a nonelitist. "Reagan seems to stop short of arousing the gutteral hatred that George Wallace or Spiro Agnew did. . . . [He] does not come across as a mean man. . . ." (Drew, 1981, p. 116).

Reagan has been described as having "a conventional mind." He is lacking in curiosity. Along the way he has arrived at his own insights "and is confident about his own judgments" (Drew, 1981, p. 116).

Reagan watchers see him as not involved in the details of government. He delegates much of the day-to-day operation of the government to others. Some see him as a shrewd but intellectually lazy leader with relaxed work habits. Unlike Jimmy Carter, he is not a worrier. His is the "politics of optimism." "Reagan's stories have happy endings; no problems are daunting" (Drew, 1985, p. 307).

Despite an extraordinary ability to appeal directly to the public and to win support for his programs, Reagan showed as early as his first Presidential campaign that he is not always prepared to discuss the programs he is espousing. As a result, he has made a number of politically damaging statements.

Reagan's advisors learned that he must be protected from the public, that his appearances and public statements must be carefully prepared in order for him to perform at his best. As I have indicated above, Ronald Reagan, the actor, communicates most effectively when reading from prepared statements. It appears that he also is good at writing his own speeches. Reagan, it is claimed, has written more of his own "scripts" than any other post-World War II President (Barrett, 1983).

Reagan enjoys extemporaneous speaking and believes that he is good at it. Early in his career he was a successful sports announcer, which required an ability to improvise. Answering reporters' questions in an extemporaneous manner, however, highlights Reagan's poor grasp of detail and his tendency to make impulsive, regrettable remarks.

REAGAN'S NEWS CONFERENCES

It is, perhaps, the need to protect Reagan from himself that led his advisors to counsel against frequent news conferences. During the first year in office, he held only six press conferences, the smallest number of any post-World War II President.

Reagan began all his news conferences with opening statements. They were well-prepared, lucid, and persuasive. Reagan's introductory remarks contained less than one *qualifier* per 1000 words, his answers to reporters' questions almost 12.

Reagan was direct, informal, and friendly with the press corps. As soon as he learned a journalist's full or first name, he used it in addressing the reporter. If we keep in mind the fact that Reagan often addressed journalists by their first names on national television, we must suppose that this practice was highly flattering to them and surely contributed to the good rapport he had with the press corps.

Although the general tone of Reagan's press conferences was serious, he did elicit a good deal of laughter with his frequent quips. Reagan showed extraordinary patience when dealing with aggressive reporters. He almost always responded in a friendly, nondefensive way to hostile questions, rarely taking offense. Much of Reagan's humor was disarming, as in the following excerpt from the March 6, 1981, news conference:

SARAH MCCLENDON: Did you mean to give a signal to other Republicans that if they don't conform, then off would go their heads?

PRESIDENT: How can you say that about a sweet fellow like me? (Public Papers of the Presidents of the United States, 1982, p. 209)

It is clear that Reagan did not avoid frequent news conferences because of poor relationships with the White House press corps. Reporters liked Reagan and tried to protect him during his Presidency. Reagan's advisors realized that the President often made impulsive statements when unprepared. These remarks were either incorrect or revealed politically damaging attitudes. The format agreed upon by Reagan and his advisors was to schedule few press conferences and to discuss important national and international issues during the carefully prepared opening remarks. The question and answer periods were singularly uninformative and served to disarm the journalists and amuse the television audience. Compared to the rather heavy and humorless Carter news conferences, Reagan's were light and entertaining.

Reagan's popularity with the reporters can be attributed to his unfailing politeness, his lack of hostility and defensiveness, and his conveying before national television audiences a sense of intimacy with them. This latter practice is highly flattering to even the most cynical journalists and has probably contributed to the good press Reagan has received even when pursuing controversial programs.

Verbal Analysis

Reagan scored rather high in the following categories: *negatives, retractors, direct references,* and *nonpersonal references.* His *expressions of feeling* and *I* scores were the lowest of all the post-World War II Presidents, his *we* score among the highest.

Reagan's habit of addressing reporters by name conveyed an impression of intimacy that was, in part, illusory. The low *I/we* ratio, the high *nonpersonal references* score, and the low *expressions of feeling* score suggest an entertainer's closeness—friendly, charming, humorous. Other than his use of *direct references*, Reagan expressed feeling primarily through his moderate use of *adverbial intensifiers*.

Compared to Presidents such as Ford and Carter, Reagan revealed little of his inner thoughts and feelings. Cool and unflappable, he made few self-disclosures. He tended to turn aside questions about his family good-humoredly, in the manner of John Kennedy and Franklin Roosevelt. When Reagan was asked by a reporter what he thought of his daughter, Maureen, running in the California Senatorial primary, he smiled, waved his hand, and said, "I hope not." That was the end of the exchange, and, apparently, the end of Maureen's senatorial aspirations.

Reagan's low *I/we* ratio not only helped diminish his expression of emotion, it also reflected the thinking and behavior of a "team player." Reagan has seen himself very much as the leader of a conservative movement rather than as a one-man administration á la Jimmy Carter. His ability to delegate authority is well-known and has been a source of strength as well as an Achilles heel of his Administration. Leaders of revolutionary movements characteristically use *we* when they do not wish to encourage a personality cult. Reagan actually used very few "imperial" *we*'s. In reading transcripts of his news conferences, one gets the impression that he was actually thinking of his aides when he said, "We believe," "We did," and so on. Reagan rarely took sole credit or blame for successes and failures. He generally gave full and enthusiastic credit to his subordinates when they were under attack, always denying allegations of wrongdoing. Although Reagan has been criticized for supporting wayward associates, it is likely that much of the public has found this show of loyalty to be an attractive trait.

Reagan's moderate *qualifiers* and rather high *retractors* scores suggest an ability to make decisions but a tendency to reverse them. During Reagan's Presidential campaign and first year in office, there were a number of examples of his blurting out remarks or making impulsive decisions that had to be reversed. This tendency has continued through his second administration, the summit meeting with Soviet Secretary Gorbachev in Iceland being a good example. Working without the participation of key arms-control experts, Reagan apparently made proposals that later had to be withdrawn as not being in the best interests of the United States. Characteristically, Reagan denied making the proposals, although the Soviet verbatim transcripts of the meetings seem to contradict him.

Reagan's use of *negatives* was quite high. Only Eisenhower had a higher score in this category. In previously tested subjects, a *negatives* score at Reagan's level indicated an oppositional streak, a certain stubbornness. Also reflected in a high *negatives* score is a possible need to deny unpleasant aspects of reality. Reagan's dogged adherence to certain positions and his unwavering loyalty to friends in legal trouble may be examples of this tendency. We shall consider below how these personality characteristics may have affected Reagan in crisis situations.

Admitting Ignorance

One of Reagan's most appealing characteristics was his ability to admit ignorance when unable to answer a reporter's question. Consider the following excerpt from the March 6, 1981 news conference:

REPORTER: Mr. President, as you well know, Turkey has been hit hard during the 3 1/2 years' arms embargo from the United States. Do you consider to increase aid to Turkey on or above the amount President Carter suggested for the fiscal year 1982 which is $700 million? And also, would you favor a military grant to Turkey?

PRESIDENT: I—this is an awful thing to confess—I can't really out of all the programs remember where that figure stands.

REPORTER: It stands, Mr. President, the $400 million is the military aid and the $300 million is the economic aid.

PRESIDENT: Yes, but I mean I can't recall where our figures stand in comparison to that, but I know that basically our philosophy is one of continued aid (Public Papers of the Presidents of the United States, 1982, pp. 210–211).

The above exchange suggests that Reagan was unprepared for the question and did not have sufficient mastery of the facts to be able to deal with it. Such situations rarely occurred during the news conferences of Carter, Kennedy, and Nixon, all of whom were on top of most issues. Eisenhower, who did not prepare carefully for news conferences, dealt with factual questions he couldn't answer by having his press secretary present to provide the requested data.

Favorite Words and Expressions

Like all post-World War II Presidents, Ronald Reagan could easily be identified by certain verbal expressions he used over and over again during his news conferences. He frequently began sentences with "Well," "And," and "So." Another interesting Reagan habit was to use "yes" parenthetically in a rhetorically effective way. In speaking of spending cuts, during the January 29, 1981 press conference, Reagan said, "And, yes, they probably are going to be bigger than anyone has ever attempted. . . ."(Public Papers of the Presidents of the United States, 1982, p. 56). Other favorite Reagan phrases were "I happen to believe," "I have to believe," and "as you know." Of all the Presidents we have studied, Reagan was most apt to use the impersonal *you*.

Reagan in Crisis Situations

How does Reagan behave in crisis situations? In our discussion of some of the other Presidents, we tried to associate verbal behavior, particularly in response to stress questions, with demonstrated behavior during administration crises. The reader is justified in being skeptical of these attempts. After all, it is not very difficult to examine past behavior and compare it with an individual's verbal style. To predict *future* crisis behavior from grammatical choices is far more challenging. In the case of Reagan, I have done just that. Prior to the Irangate crisis, I published an article in *Political Psychology* comparing the verbal styles of Jimmy Carter and Ronald Reagan. In discussing my findings, I speculated about Reagan's possible behavior under stress. With our present knowledge of Reagan's actual behavior during the Iran affair, the reader can judge to what extent the following excerpt from my published article correctly predicted Reagan's real life behavior (Weintraub, 1986):

> The President's moderate *qualifiers* and rather high *retractors* scores suggest an ability to make decisions but a tendency to reverse them. In subjects we have previously tested, a *negatives* score at Reagan's level indicates an oppositional trait and a possible need to deny unpleasant aspects of reality. Together with the previously mentioned high *retractors* score, this finding might cause concern were Reagan a loner. As the leader of a team, his impulsive steak and reluctance to look at unpleasant facts are probably neutralized by advisors who participate in decisions.

Observers of the Reagan Administration are in general agreement that the politically damaging Irangate crisis may have been, in part, caused by a changing of the White House staff after Reagan's first term. Wanting to "let Reagan be Reagan," the new advisors allowed previously restrained Presidential impulses to emerge and influence foreign policy decisions.

SUMMARY

Reagan's verbal behavior reflects the thinking of a team player, a leader who sees himself as part of a larger movement. Given to impulsive and ill-considered behavior under stress, Reagan carefully limited his appearances before the press. He communicated administration policies in prepared opening remarks. The question and answer periods were holding actions in which the President skillfully parried with the reporters, holding them off with a mixture of humor and charm.

During news conferences, Reagan was low-key and modest, sharing most of the credit for administration achievements with his subordinates. A low *I/we* ratio made Reagan appear as the leader of a team rather than as an egocentric commander. His approach to the press was direct and flattering. Reagan quickly learned the first names of the reporters and often used them when answering questions before national television audiences. Although frequently put on the spot by aggressive journalists, the President never reacted with impatience or hostility. He modestly and contritely confessed to ignorance of facts and did not attempt to defeat the press with superior knowledge of the issues as did Jimmy Carter.

A disquieting finding is a high *negatives* score, which, together with a high *retractors* score and a moderate *qualifiers* score, portrays a leader who can make decisions but is given to impulsivity, stubbornness, and a disinclination to look at unpleasant aspects of reality. The Irangate affair showed the extent to which Reagan was dependent upon the quality and unity of the people around him to avoid damaging errors in judgment.

CONCLUSION

We have come to an end of our verbal analysis of the speech patterns of post-World War II U. S. Presidents. We have learned that even during the first "honeymoon" year, when relationships between the

President and the White House journalists are most cordial, significant differences in speaking styles among the various Chief Executives emerge. In many ways, the Presidential speech patterns reflect ways of thinking and behaving that have been described by observers of the Washington scene. Thus Kennedy's coolness is reflected by a high *nonpersonal references* score, Eisenhower's warmth by high scores in the "emotional" categories, and Ford's indecisiveness by a very high *qualifiers* score.

The reader will protest that many Presidential traits of importance to the public are not reflected in their choices of grammatical structures or, at the least, are not revealed by my method of analysis. I can only answer that we are dealing with a relatively new technique, the ultimate usefulness of which should not be judged by the results achieved thus far.

Epilogue

Let us briefly review what we have accomplished in the previous chapters. In a sense, I have continued the approach begun in *Verbal Behavior*, associating choices of grammatical structures with styles of thinking and behaving. The main departure from previous practice has been to emphasize the study of the individual speaker rather than groups of speakers.

In order to provide a broader syntactic base for personality evaluation, we found it useful to identify those categories that reflect spontaneity and emotion in speech. These investigations allowed us to roam widely into such areas as political discourse, spontaneity in the theater, and the grammar of decision making and deception. In the course of our study of emotion in speech, we discovered the usefulness of *adverbial intensifiers* as a powerful marker for age and sex differences.

Exploring the problem of deception and its detection through verbal analysis proved to be a fascinating if frustrating experience. Clearly the concept of lying itself must be clarified before more refined techniques can be developed and applied to lie detection.

In approaching the difficult subject of intimate language, we were forced, for the time being, to abandon the rigorous experimental approach and rely on anecdotal data. Although a time-honored and perfectly respectable way of looking at verbal behavior, the anecdotal approach should be seen as preliminary to the more careful and systematic collection of data now taking place in the laboratory. Still, we were able, on the basis of casual observation, to raise certain hypotheses about intimacy and familiarity.

After developing a method for the analysis of individual speakers, we applied it to the speaking habits of the seven post-World War II Presidents. Careful study of their news conferences during the first year in office—"the honeymoon period"—showed significant differences in the use of almost all of our verbal categories. These differences could be rather easily associated with patterns of Presidential behavior described by biographers and political writers. What was more impressive, we were able to demonstrate that it is possible to predict, on the basis of verbal style, future Presidential behavior in crisis situations.

WHERE DO WE GO FROM HERE?

The principal obstacle in the way of more widespread use of verbal behavior analysis in clinical work is the cost of data collection and transcription. In analyzing the speech patterns of the post-World War II Presidents, I enjoyed the luxury of verbatim material provided by the Government Printing Office. In *Verbal Behavior*, I discussed at length the technical difficulties of automated verbal data collection and transcription. In the intervening years, little progress has been made. Readers who have seen television commercials demonstrating computerized word recognition systems may have been misled into believing that practical methods of automatically transcribing free speech already exist. This is not the case. Because of regional accents and idiosyncratic factors affecting pronunciation, speakers must "train" a word recognition device before it can automatically transcribe their speech. Even then the results leave much to be desired. Automatic transcription remains a development for the future.

Historical Research

If the uses of verbal behavior analysis in routine clinical work are limited, many applications of the method in historical and biographical research are possible. Our study of the Presidents has demonstrated that verbal analysis allows us to look at well-known leaders in different ways. The usefulness of our method is even more obvious in the case of little known world leaders. Most countries do not expose their leaders' personal lives to the kind of public scrutiny common in the United States. Revolutionary leaders may explode onto the scene in third-world nations with almost nothing known about them abroad. A method such as ours, which can tell us something about such leaders' personalities and styles of leadership from their speaking performances, can be of great practical use. The cost involved in analyzing the speech patterns of prominent leaders can easily be justified.

WHAT DOES IT ALL MEAN?

In the course of my verbal behavior studies, I have tried to associate my categories with psychoanalytic defense mechanisms, which they closely resemble. More recently, I have found it useful to compare grammatical choices with Chomsky's transformations. It seems highly probable that certain of my categories reflect universal human characteristics. It is difficult to imagine human beings anywhere not reasoning, qualifying, reconsidering, exaggerating, and evaluating.

Claims for universal applicability have also been made for Freudian mechanisms and for grammatical transformations. In a fascinating analysis, Campbell (1982) has even compared the importance of generative, transformational grammar to our genetic code: "A generative grammar provides in language what . . . the DNA information system provides in the cell, namely a virtually inexhaustible reservoir of possibilities" (p. 95).

How much of what we have discovered can be generalized across languages and cultures? A great deal. In my work as a consultant to the United States Government, I have analyzed translations of speech samples from a number of Western European and Middle Eastern languages. The frequency of occurrence of many of our categories—*negatives, qualifiers, retractors, explainers,* in particular—are remarkably constant, no matter what the language or the culture.

Hopefully, this book will encourage readers to think about verbal behavior. Some readers with an interest in research may develop their own hypotheses and strategies and try to answer some of the questions I have raised or ask questions that have not occurred to me. In no other discipline are more data available. The stimulus for the reader's first verbal project may be his next conversation!

APPENDIX
Scored Sample

SCORED SAMPLE

For readers interested in applying my method of verbal behavior analysis to their own research data, I have prepared a scored sample for those categories requiring judgment on the part of the scorer. Only categories discussed in this book have been scored. Three categories—*I, we,* and *me*—are scored automatically and require no special instructions. The reader should consult the scoring method outlined in Chapter I before studying the scored sample. The categories have been abbreviated as follows:

Personal references	P
Nonpersonal references	NP
Direct references	DR
Evaluators	Ev
Adverbial intensifiers	AI
Explainers	Ex
Expressions of feeling	F
Qualifiers	Q
Retractors	R
Negatives	N

Scored Sample of Free Speech

Well, I'm 21 and I go to the University of Maryland. This is my
    P   P   NP

fourth year in college. These two years I have enjoyed more than
                                        P   F

the first two years. And I have been connected more closely with
                            P

my field that I had hoped to get into. I was a day commuter for the
              P   P

first two years and lived at home. I financed my own college by
                   P   P

working during the summers and taking that money and applying

it to my college education. And then these two years have been
                                        NP

financed by the Navy Program which I am now part of. They have
                              P   NP

paid for my complete tuition, and they paid for my books. In gen-
                             NP

eral, this is a very good way of financing my last two years of
     NP   AI   Ev

school. I find this is an interesting experiment in that we have some
           NP   DR   Ex   NP

patients on our wards taping for 10 or 15 minutes during the day-

time and then writing diaries in the evening. It should be interest-
                                      NP

ing in the final study to see what the results are. I hope to be able
                          NP   P

to do this and learn a little more about the study that's being
                                  DR   NP

carried on here and in the part <u>I am functioning</u> and the rest of the
                                                    P

student nurses are functioning to contribute to it. <u>This is</u> my sec-
                    P   NP

ond month in psychiatry and <u>I have enjoyed</u> my experience there
                                    P   F

<u>very</u> much. <u>It has been</u> most interesting working with all the pa-
AI   NP

tients and <u>not</u> <u>only</u> comparing their reaction <u>but</u> also seeing how <u>I</u>
            N   AI   R

<u>react</u> to them. One of the most interesting examples <u>we have</u> <u>is</u> one
P   NP   NP

thing <u>I had</u> and <u>who seems</u> to have many compulsions. And <u>this</u>
        P   P   Q

<u>has led</u> to many feelings on part of the nursing and medical staff as
NP

to how to handle it. And <u>we were talking</u> about this today and find
                            NP

that <u>everyone is using</u> many different approaches to this. <u>Many of</u>
        NP   NP

<u>them seem to be responding</u> or be affecting him and <u>he is respond-</u>
Q   P

ing to them. But <u>it's</u> <u>very</u> interesting to find out all of the inner
                    R   NP AI

feelings of people <u>who are working</u> with him and how <u>they are</u>
                    NP   NP

<u>reacting</u> to his behavior <u>though</u> <u>I have</u> <u>only</u> had slight contact with
                                R   P   AI

him. <u>But</u> in the next week <u>I plan</u> to have more contact with him
R   P

that would—<u>since</u> that <u>will be</u> my last week on the ward. An <u>so</u> <u>I</u>
            Ex   NP   Ex

<u>can</u> also summarize on my own feelings about this young man. The
P

month that <u>I have</u> left in Psychiatry <u>I'll be spending</u> out at Spring
      P   P

Grove Mental Institution and <u>I understand</u> <u>it's</u> a <u>complete</u> different
                                  Q   NP   AI

setting there. <u>I am</u> uncertain as to my own feelings about how <u>I will</u>
            P   P

<u>accept</u> <u>only</u> half work with the patients <u>in that</u> <u>they only have</u> one
  AI   Ex   NP AI

ward meeting once a week. <u>They rarely get</u> to see their doctors
                                NP AI

except when <u>absolutely</u> necessary. <u>But</u> then again <u>it will allow</u> us to
              AI   R   NP

form new relationships to people and <u>possibly</u> in some further way
                                     Q

<u>not</u> <u>only</u> in their development and <u>possible</u> recovery <u>but</u> in our
N AI   Q   R

own development of personal relationships with other people. <u>I</u>

<u>have</u> many handy work types of hobbies of which <u>I am</u> now doing
 P   P

embroidery of which <u>I like</u> to do more of or have more time to do
                  P F

more of. <u>I'd also like</u> to have more time to do some of the knitting
        P F

and other things that <u>I do now</u>. And <u>I'm looking forward</u> to gradu-
                  P   P F

ation in June which <u>I think</u> <u>we all are</u> and be able to have some
                 Q   NP

time to do more of the other things that <u>we would like</u> to do in the
                                    NP

way of our own hobbies <u>which is</u> painting and reading—more
                        NP

along the novel line than the textbook line. And, <u>since</u> June is <u>not</u>
                                          Ex   N

<u>too</u> far off, <u>we are all very happy</u> about this. <u>I am anxious</u> to go
AI   NP   F   AI   P   F

home again next week to be able to see my family and the two

<u>lovely</u> dogs <u>we have</u> there. <u>My father's</u> presently showing one of
 Ev   P   P

the dogs and <u>I am anxious</u> to find out whether or <u>not</u> <u>he's won</u> any
           P   F   N   NP

more medals. <u>They are</u> <u>lovely</u> dogs and <u>they're</u> gray and white with
           NP   Ev   NP

black noses and ears with a pompadour type tail such as that of a

Pomeranian. <u>They only stand</u> about 18 to 20 inches high <u>but</u> re-
            NP   AI   R

semble more like a teddy bear. And <u>they're</u> <u>very</u> <u>lovable</u> dogs. And
NP   NP   AI   Ev

<u>they're</u> <u>always</u> getting into mischief. And <u>my brother grows</u> by
NP   AI   P

leaps and bounds everytime <u>I see</u> him <u>so</u> <u>this will be</u> interesting to
                            P   Ex   NP

see how much <u>he's grown</u> this time. And as for my mother, <u>it will</u>
            P   NP

<u>be</u> interesting to see what new things <u>she has started</u> at home in
                                           P

the way of projects or what local family news <u>she has gathered</u> to
                                                  P

relate to me. <u>My sister's getting married</u> the end of the month.
                    P

Therefore, I'll be making plans with her when I go home as to
   Ex   P   P

what to wear and what arrangements will have to be made. It will
                                           NP   NP

be interesting to see what arrangements she's made and what kind
                                            P

of a wedding she hopes to have and exactly what her plans are on
              P   AI   NP

her honeymoon.

TABLE A–1 Conversion of Raw Scores to Final Scores

Category*	Raw Score	Final Score
Nonpersonal References	Nonpersonal Ref. = 42	488.4
$\dfrac{\text{Nonpersonal ref.}}{\text{nonpers.} + \text{pers.}} \times 1000$	Personal ref. = 44	
Negatives	4	4.7
Direct References	2	2.3
Evaluators	4	4.7
Explainers	7	8.2
Adverbial Intensifiers	17	19.9
Feelings	8	9.4
Qualifiers	6	7.0
Retractors	7	8.2
I	34	39.8
We	7	8.2
Me	1	1.2

* All other categories are calculated my multiplying the raw score by a corrective figure. The corrective figure is obtained by dividing 1000 by the number of words and rounding off to 3 places after the decimal. Corrective figure for this protocol is $1000 \div 855 = 1.170$.

References

Albee, E. (1962). *Who's afraid of Virginia Woolf?* New York: Atheneum.

Ambrose, S.E. (1984). *Eisenhower. (Vol. II, The President)*. New York: Simon and Schuster.

Anderson, M. (1935). *Winterset*. Washington, D.C.: Anderson House.

Aronson, H., & Weintraub, W. (1967a). Sex differences in verbal behavior related to adjustive mechanisms. *Psychological Reports, 21*, 965–971.

Aronson, H., & Weintraub, W. (1967b). Verbal productivity as a measure of change in affective status. *Psychological Reports, 20*, 483–487.

Barrett, L.I. (1983). *Gambling with history: Ronald Reagan in the White House*. Garden City, New York: Doubleday and Company.

Bernstein, B. (1959). A public language: Some sociological implications of a linguistic form. *British Journal of Sociology, 10*, 311–326.

Bernstein, B. (1960). Language and social class. *British Journal of Sociology, 11*, 271–276.

Birdwhistell, R.L. (1974). Masculinity and femininity on display. In S. Weitz (Ed.), *Nonverbal communication* (pp. 144–149). New York: Oxford University Press.

Black, W.J. (1937). *The Works of William Shakespeare*. Roslyn, New York: Black's Readers Service Company.

Bradac, J.J. (1983). The language of lovers, flovers and friends: Communicating in social and personal relationships. *Journal of Language and Social Psychology, 2*, 141–162.

Campbell, J. (1982). *Grammatical Man*. New York: Simon & Schuster.

Casserly, J.J. (1977). *The Ford White House: The diary of a speechwriter*. Boulder, Colorado: Colorado Associated University Press.

Chomsky, N. (1964). Formal discussion of W. Miller and S. Ervin, "The development of grammar in child language." In U. Bellugi & R. Brown (Eds.), *The acquisition of language* (pp. 35–39). Chicago: University of Chicago Press.

Coleman, L., & Kay, P. (1981). Prototype semantics: the English word *lie. Language, 57*, 26–44.

Collier, P., & Horowitz, D. (1984). *The Kennedys: An American drama*. New York: Summit Books.

Courtright, J.A., Millar, F.E., & Rogers-Millar, L.E. (1979, August). Domineeringness and dominance: Replication and expansion. *Communication Monographs*, 46, 179–192.

DeGaulle, C. (1958, May 20). Text of news conference. *The New York Times*, p. 12.

Dolezel, L. (1980). Truth and authenticity in narrative. *Poetics Today*, 1: 7–25.

Drew, E. (1981). *Portrait of an election: The 1980 Presidential campaign.* New York: Simon and Schuster.

Drew, E. (1985). *Campaign journal: The political events of 1983–1984.* New York: Macmillan.

Dulaney, E.F. (1982). Changes in language behavior as a function of veracity. *Human Communication Research*, 9, 75–82.

Edelheit, H. (1969). Speech and psychic structure: The vocal-auditory organization of the ego. *Journal of The American Psychoanalytic Association*, 17, 381–412.

Eichler, M. (1966). The application of verbal behavior analysis to the study of psychological defense mechanisms: Speech patterns associated with sociopathic behavior. *The Journal of Nervous and Mental Disease*, 141, 658–663.

Ekman, P. (1985, October 29). Spotting lies in the workplace. *Washington Post*, p. C5.

Enkvist, N.E. (1973). *Linguistic stylistics.* The Hague: Mouton.

Fairbanks, G., and Hoaglin, L.W. (1941). An experimental study of the durational characteristics of the voice during the expression of emotion. *Speech Monographs*, 8, 85–90.

Feldstein, S. (1964). Vocal patterning of emotional expression. In J.H. Masserman (Ed.), *Science and psychoanalysis* (Vol. 7). New York: Grune & Stratton.

Ford, C.V., King, B.H., & Hollender, M.H. (1988). Lies and liars: Psychiatric aspects of prevarication. *The American Journal of Psychiatry*, 145, 554–562.

Guilford, J.P. (1965). *Fundamental statistics in psychology and education.* New York: McGraw-Hill.

Hecht, B. (1954). *A child of the century.* New York: Simon and Schuster.

Hellman, L. (1939). *The Little Foxes.* New York: Random House.

Hemingway, E. (1926). *The Sun Also Rises.* New York: Charles Scribner's Sons.

Hocking, J.E., & Leathers, D.G. (1980). Nonverbal indicators of deception: A new theoretical perspective. *Communication Monographs*, 47, 119–131.

Hopper, R., Knapp, M.L., & Scott, L. (1981). Couples' personal idioms: Exploring intimate talk. *Journal of Communication*, 31, 23–33.

Horowitz, M.W., & Newman, J.B. (1964). Spoken and written expression: An experimental analysis. *Journal of Abnormal and Social Psychology*, 68, 640–647.

Kearns, D. (1976). *Lyndon Johnson and the American dream.* New York: Harper & Row.

Kearns-Goodwin, D. (1987). *The Fitzgeralds and the Kennedys: An American saga.* New York: Simon and Schuster.

Key, M.R. (1975). *Male/female language.* Metuchen, N.J.: Scarecrow Press.

Laffal, J. (1965). *Pathological and normal language.* New York: Atherton Press.

Lalljee, M., & Cook, M. (1975). Anxiety and ritualized speech. *British Journal of Psychology*, 66, 299–306.

Lenneberg, E.H. (1964). Speech as a motor skill with special reference to nonaphasic disorders. In U. Bellugi & R. Brown (Eds.), *The acquisition of language* (pp. 115–127). Chicago: University of Chicago Press.

Mahl, G.F. (1956). Disturbances and silences in the patient's speech in psychotherapy. *The Journal of Abnormal and Social Psychology, 53,* 1–15.

Mazlish, B., & Diamond, E. (1979). *Jimmy Carter: an interpretive biography.* New York: Simon and Schuster.

Menyuk, P. (1969). *Sentences children use.* Cambridge, Mass: M.I.T. Press.

Mercer, N.M. (1976). Frequency and availability in the encoding of spontaneous speech. *Language and Speech, 19,* 129–143.

Miller, A. (1949). *Death of a Salesman.* New York: Viking.

Miller, W.L. (1978). *Yankee from Georgia: The emergence of Jimmy Carter.* New York: Times Books.

Milmoe, S., Rosenthal, R., Blane, H.T., Chafetz, M.E., & Wolf, I. (1967). The doctor's voice: Postdictor of successful referral of alcoholic patients. *Journal of Abnormal Psychology, 72,* 78–84.

Moliere, J.B. (1954). *The misanthrope* (Richard Wilbur, Trans.). New York: Harcourt, Brace & World.

Morton, A.Q. (1978). *Literary detection.* New York: Scribner.

Moskowitz, B.A. (1978). The acquisition of language. *Scientific American, 239* (5), 92–108.

Munsinger, H., & Douglass, A. (1976). The syntactic abilities of identical twins, fraternal twins, and their siblings. *Child Development, 47,* 40–50.

Natale, M., Dahlberg, C.C., & Jaffe, J. (1978). The relationship of defensive language behavior in patient monologues to the course of psychoanalysis. *Journal of Clinical Psychology, 34,* 466–470.

Ohmann, R. (1967). Prolegomena to the analysis of prose style. In S. Chatman and S.R. Levin (Eds.), *Essays on the language of literature* (pp. 398–411). Boston: Houghton Mifflin.

O'Neill, E. (1956). *Long day's journey into night.* New Haven: Yale University Press.

Public Papers of the Presidents of the United States: Dwight D. Eisenhower, 1953. Washington, D.C.: U.S. Government Printing Office, 1960.

Public Papers of the Presidents of the United States: John F. Kennedy, 1961. Washington, D.C.: U.S. Government Printing Office, 1962.

Public Papers of the Presidents of the United States: Lyndon B. Johnson, 1963–1964 (Book 1—November 22, 1963 to June 30, 1964). Washington, D.C.: U.S. Government Printing Office, 1965.

Public Papers of the Presidents of the United States: Richard Nixon, 1969. Washington, D.C.: U.S. Government Printing Office, 1971.

Public Papers of the Presidents of the United States: Richard Nixon, 1973. Washington, D.C.: U.S. Government Printing Office, 1975.

Public Papers of the Presidents of the United States: Gerald R. Ford, 1975 (Book 1—January 1 to July 17, 1975). Washington, D.C.: U.S. Government Printing Office, 1977.

Public Papers of the Presidents of the United States: Jimmy Carter, 1977 (Book 1—January 20 to June 24, 1977). Washington, D.C.: U.S. Government Printing Office, 1977.

Public Papers of the Presidents of the United States: Ronald Reagan, 1981. Washington, D.C.: U.S. Government Printing Office, 1982.

Rather, D., & Gates, G.P. (1974). *The palace guard.* New York: Harper and Row.

Reedy, G.E. (1970). *The twilight of the presidency.* New York: Mentor.

Reeves, R. (1976). *Old faces of 1976.* New York: Harper and Row.

Schlesinger, A.M., Jr. (1973). *The imperial presidency.* Boston: Houghton Mifflin.

Shapiro, T. (1979). *Clinical psycholinguistics.* New York: Plenum.

Siegel, S. (1956). *Non-parametric statistics for the behavioral sciences.* New York: McGraw-Hill.

Siegman, A.W. (1978). The meaning of silent pauses in the initial interview. *The Journal of Nervous and Mental Disease, 166,* 642–654.

Siegman, A.W., & Pope, B. (1965). Effects of question specificity and anxiety-producing messages on verbal fluency in the initial interview. *Journal of Personality and Social Psychology, 2,* 522–530.

Simon, N. (1984). *Brighton Beach Memoirs.* London: Samuel French.

Spencer, J., and Gregory, M. (1964). An approach to the study of style. In N.E. Enkvist, J. Spencer, and M.J. Gregory (Eds.), *Linguistics and Style* (pp. 57–109). London: Oxford.

Steinberg, E. (1973). *Stream of consciousness and beyond in Ulysses.* Pittsburgh: University of Pittsburgh Press.

Steingart, I., & Freedman, N. (1972). A language construction approach for the examination of self/object representation in varying clinical states. In R.R. Holt & E. Peterfreund (Eds.), *Psychoanalysis and contemporary science:* Vol. 1 (pp. 132–178). New York: MacMillan.

Vernon, M., & Miller, W.G. (1973). Language and nonverbal communication in cognitive and affective processes. In B.B. Rubinstein (Ed.), *Psychoanalysis and contemporary science:* Vol. 2 (pp. 124–135). New York: Macmillan.

Vygotsky, L.S. (1962). *Thought and language.* Cambridge, Mass.: M.I.T. Press.

Weintraub, W. (1981). *Verbal behavior: adaptation and psychopathology.* New York: Springer.

Weintraub, W. (1986). Personality profiles of American Presidents as revealed in their public statements: The Presidential news conferences of Jimmy Carter and Ronald Reagan. *Political Psychology, 7,* 285–295.

Weintraub, W., & Aronson, H. (1962). The application of verbal behavior analysis to the study of psychological defense mechanisms, Methodology and preliminary report. *Journal of Nervous and Mental Disease, 134,* 169–181.

Weintraub, W., & Aronson, H. (1964). The application of verbal behavior analysis to the study of psychological defense mechanisms, II: Speech pattern associated with impulsive behavior. *Journal of Nervous and Mental Disease, 139,* 75–82.

Weintraub, W., & Aronson, H. (1965). The application of verbal behavior analysis to the study of psychological defense mechanisms, III: Speech pattern associated with delusional behavior. *Journal of Nervous and Mental Disease, 141,* 172–179.

Weintraub, W., & Aronson, H. (1967). The application of verbal behavior analysis to the study of psychological defense mechanisms, IV: Speech pattern associated with depressive behavior. *Journal of Nervous and Mental Disease, 144,* 22–28.

Weintraub, W., and Aronson, H. (1969). Application of verbal behavior analysis to the study of psychological defense mechanisms, V: Speech pattern associated with overeating. *Archives of General Psychiatry, 21,* 739–744.

Weintraub, W., & Aronson, H. (1974). Verbal behavior analysis and psychological defense mechanisms, VI: Speech pattern associated with compulsive behavior. *Archives of General Psychiatry, 30,* 297–300.

Weintraub, W., & Plaut, S.M. (1985). Qualifying phrases as a measure of spontaneity in speech. *Journal of Nervous and Mental Disease, 173,* 694–697.

White, T.H. (1961). *The making of the President—1960.* New York: Pocket Books.

White, T.H. (1965). *The making of the President—1964.* New York: Signet Books.

Wilder, T. (1938). *Our Town.* New York: Harper and Row.

Williams, T. (1945). *The Glass Menagerie.* New York: Random House.

Winer, B.J. (1962). *Statistical principles in experimental design.* New York: McGraw-Hill.

Wouk, H. (1954). *The Caine Mutiny Court Martial.* New York: Doubleday and Company.

Index